About this Learning Guide

Shmoop Will Make You a Better Lover*
*of Literature, History, Poetry, Life...

Our lively learning guides are written by experts and educators who want to show your brain a good time. Shmoop writers come primarily from Ph.D. programs at top universities, including Stanford, Harvard, and UC Berkeley.

Want more Shmoop? We cover literature, poetry, bestsellers, music, US history, civics, biographies (and the list keeps growing). Drop by our website to see the latest.

www.shmoop.com

Table of Contents

Introduction . . . 4
In a Nutshell . . . 4
Summary . . . 4
Book Summary . . . 4
Chapter 1 . . . 6
Chapter 2 . . . 7
Chapter 3 . . . 8
Chapter 4 . . . 9
Chapter 5 . . . 10
Chapter 6 . . . 12
Chapter 7 . . . 12
Chapter 8 . . . 14
Chapter 9 . . . 15
Chapter 10 . . . 16
Chapter 11 . . . 16
Chapter 12 . . . 17
Chapter 13 . . . 18
Chapter 14 . . . 19
Chapter 15 . . . 21
Chapter 16 . . . 21
Chapter 17 . . . 22
Chapter 18 . . . 23
Chapter 19 . . . 24
Themes . . . 25
Theme of Identity . . . 25
Questions About Identity . . . 25
Chew on Identity . . . 26
Theme of Duty . . . 26
Questions About Duty . . . 26
Chew on Duty . . . 26
Theme of Lies and Deceit . . . 26
Questions About Lies and Deceit . . . 26
Chew on Lies and Deceit . . . 27
Theme of Society and Class . . . 27
Questions About Society and Class . . . 27
Chew on Society and Class . . . 27
Theme of Family . . . 27
Questions About Family . . . 28
Chew on Family . . . 28
Theme of Marriage . . . 28
Questions About Marriage . . . 28
Chew on Marriage . . . 29
Theme of Dreams, Hopes, Plans . . . 29

Questions About Dreams, Hopes, Plans . . . 29
Chew on Dreams, Hopes, Plans . . . 29
Theme of Love . . . 29
Questions About Love . . . 29
Chew on Love . . . 30
Theme of Principles . . . 30
Questions About Principles . . . 30
Chew on Principles . . . 30
Theme of Isolation . . . 31
Questions About Isolation . . . 31
Chew on Isolation . . . 31
Quotes . . . 31
Identity Quotes . . . 31
Duty Quotes . . . 35
Lies and Deceit Quotes . . . 39
Society and Class Quotes . . . 43
Family Quotes . . . 45
Marriage Quotes . . . 48
Dreams, Hopes, Plans Quotes . . . 53
Love Quotes . . . 56
Principles Quotes . . . 60
Isolation Quotes . . . 63
Plot Analysis . . . 67
Classic Plot Analysis . . . 67
Booker's Seven Basic Plots Analysis: Tragedy . . . 68
Three Act Plot Analysis . . . 69
Study Questions . . . 70
Characters . . . 71
All Characters . . . 71
Obi Okonkwo Character Analysis . . . 71
Obi Okonkwo Timeline and Summary . . . 72
Clara Okeke Character Analysis . . . 77
Clara Okeke Timeline and Summary . . . 78
Isaac Okonkwo Character Analysis . . . 79
Isaac Okonkwo Timeline and Summary . . . 80
Hannah Okonkwo Character Analysis . . . 81
Hannah Okonkwo Timeline and Summary . . . 81
Joseph Okeke Character Analysis . . . 82
Joseph Okeke Timeline and Summary . . . 82
Christopher Character Analysis . . . 83
Christopher Timeline and Summary . . . 83
Mr. William Green Character Analysis . . . 83
Mr. William Green Timeline and Summary . . . 84
Marie Tomlinson Character Analysis . . . 84
Marie Tomlinson Timeline and Summary . . . 84
Character Roles . . . 85
Character Clues . . . 86

Literary Devices 87
Symbols, Imagery, Allegory 87
Setting 89
Narrator Point of View 90
Genre 90
Tone 90
Writing Style 91
What's Up With the Title? 91
What's Up with the Epigraph? 92
What's Up with the Ending? 93
Did You Know? 94
Trivia 94
Steaminess Rating 95
Allusions and Cultural References 95
Best of the Web 96
Videos 96
Audios 96
Images 96
Documents 96

Introduction

In a Nutshell

Published in 1960, the year of Nigeria's independence, *No Longer At Ease* is the second novel in Chinua Achebe's trilogy that explores Nigeria's history through fiction. The first novel, *Things Fall Apart*, details the period leading up to "pacification," the moment when British colonizers violently took control of southern Nigeria. *No Longer At Ease* is set at the brink of Nigeria's independence, some sixty-plus years later. This second novel vividly demonstrates the moral destruction colonialism wreaked on Igbo society and culture. (The third novel in the series, *Arrow of God*, is set in the period between pacification and independence, depicting the long, slow death of Igbo culture during colonialism.)

No Longer At Ease is the story of how a young, educated Nigerian man returns home from university education abroad, certain that young men like himself *can* and *will* eliminate corruption as they replace the older, uneducated and corrupt Africans who make up the civil workforce. But due to his own pride and lack of foresight, he soon becomes involved in corruption himself. We learn how one young man, despite his pure ideals, will never be a match against a system of power that relies on corruption and bribery.

Summary

Book Summary

When *No Longer At Ease* opens, we learn pretty quickly that the main character, Obi Okonkwo, is on trial for corruption and bribery. The judge and the audience alike wonder how such a promising young man could have made bad choices. Obi, whose mother has recently died and whose engagement to Clara has just ended, feels tears spring to his eyes. The novel then backtracks in time and tells the story of how Obi ended up in such a horrible situation.

We go back to Obi's return to Nigeria from England, where he was receiving an education at a British university. Obi meets Clara on the boat back to Nigeria. They spark up a relationship quickly, and by the time Obi has gotten a job in the civil service, they are in love. Obi's return is marked by fanfare; the Umuofia Progressive Union, which gave him a scholarship (more like a loan) to go to school, throws a huge party and welcomes him back as their local hero. In fact, the expectation is that Obi's repayment of his debt will allow them to send others to school, and his position in the civil government will place the whole region of Umuofia in a position of power within government. Through Obi, they may be able to get jobs. This expectation is seen as part of helping a member of his extended family, and accepting bribes is understood to be a necessary evil.

But Obi has other plans. He has no desire to play the role of the corrupt civil servant, accepting bribes in order to help others achieve their dreams of getting a scholarship or getting jobs. It is at this point that we begin to see how Obi differentiates himself from his kinsmen. He believes that African cultures will necessarily succumb to the "superior" cultural ideas, values, and systems of Europe and the West. This isolates him from his kinsmen and his family.

Obi begins to pay a monthly sum to the Umuofia Progressive Union to pay back his school loan, and he begins to send his parents a monthly sum of money, as well as pay for his brother's school fees and his mother's hospital fees when she is sick. Soon enough, Obi's finances are stretched beyond their capacity. It's partly that Obi doesn't plan well, but it's also partly that, in addition to meeting all the duties to the Union and to his family, he's expected to live a lifestyle becoming to his social status and government position.

Soon, Obi finds he doesn't have enough money to keep up. First, he buys Clara's engagement ring after she admits that she's *osu* and so he will never be able to marry her. (It's forbidden in Igbo culture to marry an *osu*, since the *osu* class is dedicated to a particular god.) Obi gives Clara an engagement ring and then considers that they are engaged. Then, after he turns down Mr. Mark's offer of money to make sure Mr. Mark's sister Elsie appears before the Scholarship Board (and then turns down Elsie's offer to sleep with him for the same favor), Obi discovers that he needs forty pounds to pay for his car insurance. He hadn't even realized that there was an annual car insurance fee. So he goes to get a bank loan of fifty pounds. That night, Clara gets mad because he hadn't asked for her help.

The next day, however, Clara sends Obi fifty pounds and tells him to go pay the bank back. He doesn't, thinking perhaps he can make her take it back, knowing she'll insist that he keep it. Obi doesn't really want to give back the loan from Clara. The two make up and go dancing. Sounds like it'll be fine, right? It turns out that luck is just not with Obi. (Obi's friend Joseph would say he's challenged his personal god, his *chi*, to a wrestling match, and that's something you should never ever do unless you *want* to lose.) While they are dancing, somebody enters their unlocked car and steals Clara's fifty pounds.

So now Obi owes Clara fifty pounds, and he still owes the bank fifty pounds. To top it off, his mother becomes so ill that she has to go to the hospital. Since Obi's parents live on the money Obi sends them, it's obvious who will be responsible for the hospital bill. Also, his father has indicated that there is something "serious" he wants to discuss with Obi. Obi realizes that the news of Clara – and her status as *osu* – has finally reached his parents.

Obi takes a two weeks' leave from his job. The job pays him twenty-five pounds for his leave, and Obi decides to pay for his brother's school fees out of that money, realizing that if he doesn't pay it now when he has the money, he won't have it in a few months when it's due. At home, Obi's parents confront him about his engagement to Clara. Though Obi's parents raised him as Christian, and though they shunned many aspects of Igbo culture up to that point, now his father simply insists he cannot marry Clara. He says that though Christians must give up part of their indigenous culture and beliefs when they convert, this is not one of those things – it runs too deep in Igbo culture.

The reality is that Clara and her family are taboo. If Obi marries her and has children, what will happen to those children, socially and culturally? Obi may *feel* that the time is ripe to end certain cultural customs, but he has failed to understand how some traditions are so important to people that they cannot change overnight. Obi may *feel* isolated from his culture and kinsmen due to his education and his social status, but he is surrounded. He can't escape his culture, the judgments of his people, or their expectations. And worst of all, Obi's mother tells him that if he marries Clara while she is still alive, she will kill herself.

Obi returns to Lagos in an agitated state of mind. Who wants to be responsible for their mother's suicide? He tells Clara that they must just lay low, but Clara understands what he isn't saying – that his parents will never accept their relationship. She breaks up with him. That's when Obi discovers she's pregnant. So now, he decides that he has to borrow money to pay for an abortion. When Clara is hospitalized due to an infection from the abortion procedure, Obi realizes that he has made a mistake. He sends Clara a letter and begs her to come back to him. But it is too late. Clara returns his letter unopened and she leaves Lagos soon after. Then his mother dies, and Obi sends all the money he can to pay for her funeral, but he stays in Lagos and doesn't go home for her funeral.

With Clara gone, and his mother gone, Obi sinks into a deep depression. He begins to let go of his former convictions. Apparently, it was Clara who kept Obi on the straight and narrow all along. Deeply in debt, with no one to keep him steady, and mourning his mother's death, Obi forsakes all his lofty principles and begins to accept bribes left and right. But he does maintain a certain semblance of principles – he refuses to accept bribes from people who don't have the minimum qualifications to appear before the Scholarship Board. Because he only accepts bribes from people who are going to appear before the Board anyway, he gets a reputation for following through on his bribes.

At last, Obi is caught accepting a bribe and found guilty at his trial.

Chapter 1

- Mr. Obi Okonkwo enters the courtroom for his trial.
- One of his lawyers is late – his car broke down on the way – and gets a reprimand from the judge.
- The courtroom is full of idle spectators, all anxious to hear the verdict.
- Obi himself is indifferent, until the moment when the judge asks how such a promising young man could have done what Obi did.
- Obi feels the sting of tears in his eyes. He had prepared for this moment, and planned to avoid crying, but now he is unable to help himself.
- We then leave the courtroom and jump to the club bar. Mr. Green, Obi's boss, has a drink at the club bar after playing tennis. He strikes up a conversation with a British Council man.
- The British Council man says he doesn't understand why Obi "did it."
- But Mr. Green knows why: he claims that Africans are thoroughly corrupt. All the education in the world, he says, doesn't change that fact.
- In Lagos, the Umuofia Progressive Union holds an emergency meeting. Umuofia is Obi Okonkwo's hometown and the Union is meeting to discuss Obi's case again.
- They quibble over the facts of the case again: they gave him 800 pounds to study in England but he ruins himself over a girl. Should they continue to support him, since he is a brother, or should they let the case go?

- What they don't understand, most of all, is how he could get *caught*.
- Most people don't accept bribes themselves. They go through other people, so that it can never be traced to them.
- Everyone now wonders how Obi could have acted so foolishly? What good *was* that college education if he does things like this?
- Ultimately they decide that it is not their desire to wish harm on others, but if a man wishes harm on them, then they don't mind if he is ruined.
- The implication is clear: Obi is such a man.
- We then go back to the time when the Obi's village decided to send him get an education.
- After the village of Umuofia had scraped together the money to send one of their citizens to get a college education in England, Obi had been the village's first choice. His grades were the highest in his province.
- When Obi went to England, everybody in Umuofia got excited.
- The priest at the Anglican Church quoted a Bible verse about Jesus to show that this was the fulfillment of prophecy – that somehow Obi would help his people.
- Obi's father, Isaac, threw a huge feast.
- The pastor told Obi that in the past, the village would have required him to be a fighter, a man of military prowess, to protect the village. Instead, the pastor went on, Obi would help his village by bringing knowledge back to them.
- The women, led by Mary, sang hymns, said goodbye to Obi, and sent him on his way – having sacrificed a great deal to pay for his education.

Chapter 2

- This chapter skips around in the past, but effectively takes us through the four years Obi Okonkwo spent in England.
- During that time, Obi finally learned what Nigeria meant to him – it is home.
- But when he returned, it wasn't to the Nigeria he had remembered or imagined during his exile.
- Before he left for England, he had spent a few days with his friend Joseph in Lagos.
- It was his first trip to Lagos and his impression of the city had been formed by soldiers who had visited his village when he was young and told tales about electricity and the omnipotence of the white man, who could do everything except create human beings.
- Joseph told Obi all about film and dancing and politics. Most important, he told Obi all about women – and how loose they were in Lagos. On an outing with Joseph, he sees a heavily made-up woman on a Lagos street. He doesn't like the way she looks.
- When Obi returns several years later, he finds himself waiting for his girlfriend Clara in one of poorer neighborhoods in Lagos. He notices the same vibrant life juxtaposed to the dirty smells of the city and he realizes, "This is the real Lagos."
- Obi recalls a poem he'd written during his time in England, a nostalgic poem about the beauty of Nigeria and the laziness of rural life – and he realizes with disgust that his poem bears little resemblance to the dirty street scene confronting him now.
- As he drives away, Obi almost hits a man on a bike who is carrying a bag that proclaims his career of choice: FUTURE MINISTER.

- As they drive away to the sterile, formerly white neighborhood where Obi lives, Obi and Clara fight because Clara wanted to go to the movies and Obi didn't want to go.
- We see their problematic relationship in the way they negotiate what they want: Clara refuses to directly ask for what she wants. Obi says no but after Clara sulks, he pretends to surrender, to do what she wants, knowing she won't make him do it.
- We get the sense that their relationship seems based on doing things they don't want to do. Clara listens to the poems he reads, spends time with his friends when she doesn't want to.
- For example, she suffers through a lunch with Obi's friend Christopher, who talks politics with Obi.
- Obi argues that corruption in Nigeria's political scene is a result of experienced but uneducated men taking the top posts. They worked their way to the top through bribery. He thinks a university educated man with even just a little bit of experience is better suited to fill those posts and less corruptible. Because education allows them to go to the top more quickly, they don't *need* to bribe their way.
- As they talk, Clara calls Zacchaeus, Obi's cook, and requests more soup. Zacchaeus obeys but resents it.

Chapter 3

- We now get the story of how Obi and Clara met.
- Obi and Clara first met at a dance in England. Obi fell in love immediately and asked her to dance, but he was so awkward that she ran away as soon as the dance ended.
- A year and a half later, they met again when they returned to Nigeria on the same boat.
- Obi was thrilled to see her and reminded her of their first meeting. She was *not* thrilled to see him and ignored him.
- The next day, he ignores her at breakfast. But soon, he is stricken with seasickness and Clara becomes his ministering angel when she brings him medicine.
- Throughout that night, he thought of nothing else but Clara – and his infatuation is obvious the next morning when he opens the door and sees her. He realizes she had medicine for all the passengers, but because she had spoken to him in Igbo, it seemed like she had singled him out specifically.
- Obi becomes friends with Macmillan when Macmillan falls on deck and is able to laugh about it. Obi explains that Igbo names have meanings and are frequently a sentence. It turns out that both Macmillan and Obi are 25, and they wonder aloud how old Clara is. Obi guesses she's about 23, and the two men agree that she's beautiful.
- The boat anchors in the Madeiras, and Obi, Macmillan, and Clara disembark.
- They explore the city together. Macmillan buys cheap curios and Clara teases him that his girlfriend won't like it.
- When they return to the ship, Macmillan is holding Clara's right hand and Obi holds her left hand.
- On board, Macmillan heads to his cabin to write letters and Obi urges Clara to stay and keep him company. When they hear Macmillan's door close, Obi kisses her over and over and whispers, "I love you." Clara refuses to believe it but returns his kisses.

- Mrs. Wright interrupts them, claiming she has indigestion.

Chapter 4

- There was no crowd waiting for the boat when they arrived in Lagos.
- When the customs boy tries to collect a duty on Obi's radiogram, Obi asks for a receipt.
- The boy offers to reduce the fee but there will be no receipt and Obi claims he will call a policeman.
- Here we see the first example of Obi's refusal to be corrupted or to play the game of bribery.
- The Umuofia Progressive Union throws a huge welcome-home reception for Obi. Everybody is dressed up for it – everybody, that is, except Obi. This is his first mistake. People expected an educated young man to be dressed properly.
- The Secretary of the Union welcomes Obi back. He speaks of the great honor it is to have an educated son of Umuofia. He speaks of the education-loan arrangement, called the Umuofia Scholarship Scheme, where the recipient (in this case, Obi) will repay his debt to the Union in four years so that they can send other students to study in England.
- The audience loves the fluent and flowery speech.
- Obi's second mistake: he gets up and speaks plainly, using plain English, and speaks only of the value of education and how important it is to have educated men who can help lead the future independent Nigeria.
- Afterwards, some of the men ask Obi whether he has a job yet. Obi admits he does not but he has an interview. The Vice-President says that things will work out because Obi is educated, otherwise, he would have advised Obi to do some bribing to ensure getting a job.
- The President says that the men Obi is dealing with are white and won't take bribes.
- The Vice President laughs at his foolishness and claims that whites are among the most corrupt these days.
- Joseph and Obi go to dinner at a little restaurant owned by Syrians who, Joseph claims, own everything these days.
- Obi says he wants Nigerian food and Joseph says he'll arrange for his cook to make him something tomorrow.
- The white manageress comes out and complains about a duster that somebody left out. She spills some milk on herself and then sits down near her parrot. Obi watches in fascination.
- Obi says he thinks the restaurant is owned by the British, since she is British.
- He also tells Joseph that he doesn't want to stay in the hotel that the Union has put him up in –he wants to stay with Joseph.
- Joseph wonders if that seems proper since, after all, Obi is educated. But Obi doesn't care what people think.
- The talk turns to the idea of "destiny" and Obi and Joseph reminisce about how obvious it was, when they were growing up, that Obi would end up going to college in England. They even laugh about the letter he wrote to Hitler when he was young.
- When they leave the restaurant, the Minister of State – the Honorable Sam Okoli – walks

into the room. Obi is transfixed but not by the Hon Sam Okoli.
- He's transfixed by Clara, who is sitting in the Minister's car.

Chapter 5

- Within a month of returning home, Obi encounters two examples of the kind of corrupt African that he had been criticizing: the uneducated African who gets to the top through bribery.
- He meets this first corrupt African at the Public Service Commission when he goes for his job interview.
- As part of the interview, Obi discusses tragedy in literature with the Chairman of the Commission, a "fat jolly" Englishman. Obi argues that suicide is not a tragedy. Real tragedy is suffering without relief. When a life does consist of endless suffering, no one else even knows because this kind of suffering often happens off to the side.
- The Chairman asks if anybody on the Board has questions for Obi.
- The African member who had been sleeping wakes up and asks Obi if his real motive for seeking a job in the civil service is to take bribes.
- Enraged, Obi replies that this is an impossible question to answer because wouldn't a person who intended on taking bribes lie to the board about it?
- At home, when Joseph tells Obi he shouldn't have gotten angry since he needs the job, Obi refers to this as the "colonial mentality."
- Essentially, Joseph responds that Obi is tempting fate. (What he actually says is that Obi shouldn't "challenge his *chi* to a wrestling match," but that idiom essentially means that he shouldn't tempt fate.)
- The two friends discuss Joseph's impending marriage, and the bride-price he paid his bride's family. Joseph tells Obi that because of his higher salary, Obi will likely pay four times as much as Joseph paid.
- Obi claims that he will refuse to pay a bride-price at all.
- Joseph jokes that Obi must intend to be a priest then and never marry.
- While waiting to find out if he has a job, Obi visits his hometown of Umuofia. He catches a ride on a mammy wagon with other passengers.
- On the way, they're stopped by a policeman. When the driver's mate tries to bribe the policeman, Obi looks his way and the policeman, not willing to risk it in case Obi is a government official, pretends he's offended by the very idea.
- The driver continues for a while, but then stops just up the road and asks Obi why he looked at the policeman. Obi says the police officer has no right to take a bribe. The driver responds that this incident makes him unwilling to give rides to educated people in the future.
- Then Obi realizes that they stopped because the driver's friend had run back and given the policeman a bribe after all.
- During the rest of the trip, Obi wonders what it will take to change Nigerian society so it is not so corrupt.
- Then he turns his mind to wondering why Clara doesn't want him to tell his family about her, and whether that means she isn't sure if she wants to marry him.

* He feels sleepy and begins to think erotic thoughts, but finds it interesting that he can say anything in English but can only *think* dirty words in Igbo.
* Two of the other passengers begin to sing a song about a man killing his in-law. Obi tries to make sense of the song, since killing an in-law (who is your *chi*, or your personal god) is one of the worst things you can do.
* Obi's homecoming in Umuofia is a grand affair, with a "pleasure" car driving him from the village of Onitsha to Umuofia, and musicians waiting to serenade him into the village when he arrives. The whole village descends on Mr. Okonkwo's compound for the celebration.
* Some of the citizens criticize Isaac Okonkwo, a Christian, for failing to do his cultural duty – that is, take a sacrifice to the chief rainmaker in Umuofia for the return of his so, Obi.
* Meanwhile, Isaac Okonkwo has an argument with some of the men in the village about rainmaking.
* One of the old men tells Isaac that because nobody in the village of Umuofia had been killed by lightning, it is proof that the work their forefathers had done to protect the village and its inhabitants from lightning was powerful and effective.
* Isaac argues that Nwokeke, who survived a lightning strike the year before, should not have been hit by lightning if it was truly working.
* But the old man tells Isaac that Nwokeke had been hit in another village, so that the lightning must have mistaken him for a citizen of that other village.
* Throughout his time in England, Obi had been terribly homesick for Umuofia. He's proud of his people as they welcome him home in such splendor and joy.
* They marvel at how far Obi has traveled – to England and back – and on the water.
* They suggest that Obi has visited the land of the spirits and they must break a kola nut.
* Isaac objects, since his is a Christian home; here they do not sacrifice kola nut to idols.
* Ogbuefi Odogwu says he has a kola nut they can use, and they can break it the Christian way.
* Isaac brings three kola nuts, claiming he didn't wish to refuse them a kola nut, he just didn't want to see it offered to idols.
* Odogwu adds his kola nut to Isaac's. He blesses it in the name of Jesus Christ, and Isaac teases him that he should become a Christian. Odogwu says he will, if he is made pastor.
* The men discuss the educated Africans who return from England with a white wife; they are glad Obi didn't do that, since it divides and separates families.
* Obi is proud when they congratulate him for maintaining his cultural heritage, and his pride of being black and remaining black.
* Odogwu claims that Obi, the grandson of Ogbuefi Okonkwo (the tragic hero of *Things Fall Apart*) is Ogbuefi Okonkwo returned in the flesh.
* Isaac doesn't appreciate this comment and claims dead men don't return.
* But Odogwu has already made up his mind. He goes on to say that greatness is no longer in the things they treasured in the past, like titles or having many wives and children. These days, he says, greatness is found in the white man's culture. And most importantly, he says, greatness is not something you choose – it chooses you.

Chapter 6

- Obi's homecoming is marred by his mother's illness, and the fact that both his parents are obviously poverty-stricken to the point of hunger.
- It was terrible, he thought, that the church didn't take better care of them, after all the years of service his father had given.
- That night obi and his father talk.
- Isaac says he had been afraid he would die before Obi returned. The next day, he says, they'll go worship God together at the church.
- Obi wonders what Isaac would say if he knew that Obi was now an atheist. Obi lies and reassures Isaac that he read the Bible while he was in college.
- The family gathers for prayers and Scripture reading. Obi watches his mother and wonders if, despite her identity as an apparently devout Christian woman, she might have gravitated towards traditional culture if she weren't married to his father. (Isaac was a catechist who believes his responsibility is to uphold Christian virtues and tradition, and to let go of the parts of their culture that the missionaries condemned, such as eating food offered to idols and telling folk tales.)
- Though his mother had tried to follow his father's commands, there were times when she slipped up. For example, when Obi was embarrassed at school because he didn't know any of the folk tales common in the village, she told him some tales so he could participate in class.
- He remembers how he was told a story of a clever sheep that hid her baby lambs in some palm-kernels when she went to the market. The leopardess that came looking for the baby lambs was unsuccessful in her hunt, then thoroughly startled when she cracked the palm-kernels open and they ran away into the forest.
- Obi tells his father that he will pay his younger brother John's school fees. Then they go to bed.
- Obi takes a long time to fall asleep as he thinks about his responsibilities to his parents.
- He decides he will give them ten pounds a month from his salary, and wishes he didn't have to pay the Umuofia Progressive Union twenty pounds a month.
- He thinks about Clara and wonders again why she didn't want him to tell his parents about them. He thinks his mother, who once told him she could not die until she saw his first-born child, will be thrilled to see him settle down and get married.
- He falls asleep listening to a heavy rain.

Chapter 7

- Obi's first day at work reminded him of his first day of school.
- On that particular day many years ago, the Inspector of Schools, Mr. Jones, arrived unannounced. Mr. Jones wasn't pleased with something the headmaster, Simeon Nduka, had done and yelled at him. But when he tried to slap Nduka, who had been an excellent wrestler as a young man, he quickly ended up on his back.
- Mr. Green, Obi's boss, greeted him by saying that he'd be okay in his job if he wasn't too lazy and if he used his brain. Then he chastised the Administrative Assistant, Mr. Omo, for

not doing something. Mr. Omo turned around and chewed out a junior assistant.

- Obi was shadowing Mr. Omo that day and he decided he didn't like Mr. Green and that Mr. Omo was one of the "old" kind of Africans he had been criticizing, incompetent and prone to corruption.
- Mr. Green called for Obi at that moment and asked Obi if he had received a formal offer. When Obi says no, Mr. Green tells him that he is supposed to use the word *sir* when talking to superiors. Then he hangs up the phone.
- Obi buys a nice car – a Morris Oxford – a week later when he learns that he has enough credit to buy a car as a civil servant. And he gets sixty pounds to buy new clothes. So he takes Clara out in style for drinks at the Hon. Sam Okoli's house.
- Obi liked the Hon. Sam Okoli, who wasn't trying to seduce Clara away from him.
- As they have drinks, Okoli shows Obi his new recording machine and shows how he can use it to record their entire conversation.
- Into the recorder, Okoli makes a comment about how the white man doesn't belong in Nigeria. He adds that he had a Nigerian assistant who was not smart, but now he has an assistant who is a white man and says "sir" when he talks to Okoli. "Our people have a long way to go," Okoli concludes.
- On the way home, Clara is clearly upset about something and Obi works hard to get her to confide in him.
- In the past, when Obi told a girl he loved her, half of him was whispering that he was being silly. But with Clara, he really loved her, with his whole being.
- Clara tells him that he can't marry him. And then, sobbing, she finally admits why: she is an *osu*.
- Obi tells her not to be ridiculous.
- Joseph wakes up when Obi gets home and Obi tells him that Clara is an *osu*.
- Joseph tells him not to worry, that he found out in time, before he actually married her.
- But Obi insists that he's going to marry Clara after all.
- Joseph is shocked and says Obi must not know what an *osu* is but Obi stubbornly insists that he knows "more" about *osus* than Joseph himself. Joseph gives up and goes to bed.
- Obi thinks to himself that it is about time that the concept of *osu* is abolished in the modern Nigeria. (An *osu* is a person that has been dedicated to serving a god; that person's descendents are part of a "forbidden caste" and can't marry non- *osu*)
- The next day, Obi takes Clara to Kingsway to buy an engagement ring and, at Clara's prompting, a Bible to go with the ring.
- At home, Joseph asks how Clara was, and Obi tells him how he and Clara tried to have a private conversation in the car.
- They parked it and sent the driver away. But they were alone for only a few minutes when a policeman arrived and assumed that Clara was a prostitute and they were in the car for a good time. Then Obi tells Joseph that he and Clare are now engaged.
- Joseph tells him to think more carefully about this. Obi's decision concerns not just himself but all his descendents and, in fact, his entire family. His decision to marry an *osu* will make his family outcasts as well. Perhaps in the future, marriages of these kinds will be possible but for now, they clearly are not.
- But Obi says that he is just being a pioneer.
- Joseph says that his decision will also anger and shame the men and women who gave money so that Obi could be educated in England.
- Obi knows that his family will oppose his marriage to an *osu*. He thinks his only hope is if

he convinces his mother that it's a good idea.

Chapter 8

- Obi misses the November meeting of the Umuofia Progressive Union, but he picks up Joseph and takes him to the December meeting in style (i.e., in a fancy, new car).
- Before Obi arrives, Joseph tells his co-workers that his "brother" has studied the Classics in England – a small lie, since Obi studied English, but Joseph thinks "Classics" sounds more impressive.
- Joseph adds that Obi works as the Secretary to the Scholarship Board. His co-workers mention that he must be a wealthy man, since every student who wants to study in England will go visit him in his house – i.e., bring him a bribe – and Joseph responds that Obi doesn't take bribes. His co-workers fail to believe him.
- The entire Umuofia Progressive Union is impressed when Joseph and Obi arrive in Obi's new car. But after a few exclamations, the meeting continues.
- The problem they are discussing is the fact that Joseph Udo got fired because he was sleeping on the job.
- Joshua's boss had never received the ten-pound bribe that Joshua had promised him, and so he found an excuse to get rid of him. Now Joshua needs another ten pounds to find a new job. The Union agrees to it. But then another member mentions that money is not enough; everybody needs to find out if there is an opening where they are working. In other words, bribes alone are insufficient, connections are equally important.
- Then they discuss the complaints the young people had about Obi's reception. They had not received any of the beer that was bought for the occasion; instead, they were forced to drink Lagos palm wine, which is no better than water.
- Obi gets up to speak. He asks for a small delay of four months before he starts paying back his loan; he has been gone for four years and now has many small matters to take care of before he can begin to pay back the scholarship.
- It is clear that some members of the Union are amenable to a four-month grace period, while others are not.
- The President of the Union gets up to speak. He asks Obi to consider a couple of things: his monthly salary is more than many of the members of the Union make in one year. Adding insult to injury, he says has heard that Obi is running around with a girl of "doubtful ancestry."
- Obi is furious and starts yelling at the President that he should take him to court.
- The President responds that he can take him to court, but let him finish what he is saying.
- Obi says he won't listen to him any more. Furthermore, he's sorry he asked for a grace period of the loan and he will now start paying it immediately.
- He runs off, despite some of the men's attempts to stop him. He gets in his car and tells his driver to leave immediately. Joseph also tries to stop him but Obi tells him to get away. He orders his driver to take him to Clara's house.

Chapter 9

- Obi strikes up a friendship with Mr. Green's pretty English secretary, Miss Tomlinson, who is constantly criticizing her boss behind his back.
- Obi thinks it's possible she's a "plant" intended to get him in trouble but soon he finds himself responding to her overtures of friendship. When he introduces Miss Tomlinson to Clara, Miss Tomlinson is very friendly and talks about nothing but how beautiful Clara is for the rest of the day. Obi decides he likes Miss Tomlinson a lot.
- A gentleman comes to see Obi. His name is Mr. Mark and he hopes that Obi can put in a good word for his sister, who wants to apply for a scholarship to go study in England. He tries to be discreet in offering Obi a bribe, but Obi – who is still convinced that he can remain uncorrupt and pure – quickly gets rid of him. He pretends he doesn't know what Mr. Mark is talking about and bids him good-day.
- Obi is excited by how easy it was to say no to a bribe, and how easy it was to get rid of Mr. Mark.
- This feeling reminds Obi of the first time he had sex; the woman told him she felt "like she had been attacked by a tiger" (9.41).
- He feels like a tiger now, and reflects about how easy it is to remain pure and aboveboard. But though it is easy, he realizes that there is some temptation, since he finds it harder to live on the 47 pounds leftover after he sends 20 to the Union and another 10 to his parents. In fact, he wonders how he would find money to pay for his brother John's school fees for the upcoming term.
- Later that day, Obi hears a taxi pull up outside his apartment and wonders who it could be. Not Clara, who is working. Maybe Joseph. Obi had stopped visiting Joseph since the December Union meeting, and Clara didn't want to see Joseph ever again.
- But it is not Joseph. It is a young pretty girl: Elsie Mark. She apologizes that her brother came to his office.
- Elsie is here to make sure she is selected to appear before the Board, so that she can have a shot at getting the scholarship. She says that although her grades are good, she knows she will never have a chance of getting it unless she sees all the members at home. She tells Obi that she will do whatever he asks, if he will help her.
- Obi says he doesn't know what he can do. At that moment, Clara comes rushing in. She sees Elsie, asks how she is doing, then establishes that she is mistress of Obi's heart by asking Obi if he liked the soup she made.
- Miss Mark says she needs to go.
- Obi gives her a lift to town. On the way back home, Clara apologizes for arriving and ruining Obi's good time.
- When Obi explains Mr. Mark's visit, and Miss Mark's visit, Clara says he was too hard on Mr. Mark.
- Bribing with money, Clara says, is not as bad as bribing with one's body. Yet he treated Mr. Mark badly, and gave Miss Mark a drink and a lift back to town.

Chapter 10

- Mr. Green had warned Obi that every year he would have to pay 40 pounds for insurance on his car.
- Obi forgot his advice until the day arrived when he had to pay those 40 pounds and did not have enough in the bank.
- Obi tries to call in his debts, starting with Charles, a messenger in the department, who owes Obi thirty shillings. But Charles doesn't have it so Obi goes to the bank manager and asks for an overdraft.
- Obi goes over his financial situation in his mind. He hasn't lived lavishly, but he has had a lot of expenses.
- For example, his mother had been in the hospital the month before and he had paid the hospital the bill of 35 pounds.
- He now wishes he had gotten that grace period from the Union, but the past was the past.
- Obi reasons that he makes a lot of money, and shouldn't resent the 20 pounds that he had to give each month to repay the Union for his Scholarship.
- Yet at the same time, what the Union didn't understand was that once it put a man in the civil service, that man had to live according to his career's lifestyle.
- He had to have a car, but that meant other expenses, like insurance, and maintenance, and paying the driver's salary.
- So he borrows 50 pounds from the bank, only to return to the office and find another bill, his electricity bill. He feels like crying.
- He realizes he has other expenses, too. For example, the car needs new tires.
- And, the narrator tells us, he still doesn't know about the income tax that will be due in six months.
- After lunch, Obi tells his steward that he needs to start saving money, so he suggests little changes to the way they do things, such as cold baths from now on, less meat in the soup.
- He fights with Clara that evening, but finally admits that he's stressed about money.
- She is hurt that he didn't tell her earlier and starts to read. He tells her she's rude. She is even more hurt and continues reading. Finally, he leaves.
- At home, he looks at Clara's picture and tries to read some poetry. Instead, he found a nostalgic poem he'd written about Nigeria when he was homesick in England. It makes him smile.

Chapter 11

- Obi Okonkwo and Marie Tomlinson now know each other on a first-name basis.
- They discuss many things, especially Mr. Green.
- Marie relates Mr. Green's racist statements to Obi, and Obi responds with his own gossip about Mr. Green.
- Obi realizes that although he dislikes Mr. Green, he thinks Mr. Green has some good qualities, like his work ethic.
- It almost seems like he's working towards a deadline, though Obi isn't sure what that deadline could be, unless it's Nigeria's independence.

- Obi thinks Mr. Green is an interesting fellow, and knows that the man loves Africa. But Obi thinks the Africa he loves is the colonial version of a life of leisure, perhaps the missionary version of converting the savage heathen.
- Obi thinks about Mr. Green in the context of Conrad's *Heart of Darkness* and he decides that if Mr. Kurtz was drawn to the darkness and decline of Africa and civilization, then Mr. Green was the kind of person who had hope for a glorious future, bright possibilities on the horizon. He decides Mr. Green would make a good character in a tragedy novel, one that he should write.
- He gets a package from Clara later that morning and immediately, he is nervous – sure that it contains her engagement ring. But it is just money, no ring. Clara tells him she is sorry about the night before and that he should go cancel the overdraft.
- With tears in his eyes, Obi looks up and sees Marie watching him. But he tells her nothing is the matter.
- He wonders how Clara had managed to come up with so much money. And on the way home, he tries to think of ways to convince her to take her money back. But he's afraid he'll hurt her feelings, so he thinks of different lies he might be able to tell that would convince her to take the money back.
- Obi often imagined these scenarios in his head, whenever he knew he was going to have a difficult conversation with Clara. But they never worked in real life the way they did in his head.
- In fact, he tells her that the bank manager was pleased to be paid back so quickly.
- Finally, he tells her he didn't go to the bank, that he can't possibly take so much money from her. But when she says that she'll take the money back, Obi embraces her instead.
- They visit Christopher that night. He has a girl with him, Bisi. When he tries to introduce Clara as Obi's fiancée, Clara tells him to shut up; apparently, she's not ready for that to be public knowledge yet.
- They all go dancing at a fancy place. The couple has a good time dancing, listening to the music, people watching, and forget all about the money they left in the glove box. Bisi doesn't want to leave when they decide to go at two in the morning.
- That's when they discover they forgot to lock one of the doors. And of course, upon returning to the car, they find out that Clara's money is gone.
- Obi gets out of the car and stares at the ground. Clara gets out and holds his trembling hand, opens the door for him, and says they should leave.

Chapter 12

- Obi's father sends a letter to ask Obi to come home for a visit, not only to visit his mother, who is ill in the hospital, but also to discuss an urgent matter.
- Obi realizes that means they have finally heard about Clara, and know she is an *osu*.
- At work, Obi is distracted by the letter, no matter how hard he tries to forget it. He starts to call Clara, then hangs up and watches as Mr. Green dictates a letter to Marie.
- Then Mr. Green turns to Obi and tells him that he doesn't understand the "so-called educated Nigerian," who has unrealistic expectations that his government job should give him great luxury, not only for himself, but also for his girlfriend.

- What is this education for? So that the educated can become even greedier?
- Obi calls Christopher and they go to play tennis with two teachers, Nora and Pat, at a local convent. Two weeks earlier, they had gone out with the girls, dancing and kissing. (Note: Obi loves Clara but it doesn't stop him from making out with a white girl.) This had been followed by a couple of tennis dates.
- But today, when they arrive at the convent, they are greeted by a grim-faced Mother. They go upstairs where the girls are having tea, but it is awkward. They have tea together but the girls ignore Christopher and Obi's tennis rackets. Finally, they admit that they can't go out with them; the Mother had chided them about hanging out with African men. It was better if they didn't come again.
- On the way home, they stop to see Christopher's other girlfriend Florence, who is about to leave for England to study nursing. But she is gone, so they try Bisi. She is also out.
- Christopher wonders whether he should try to convince Florence not to go to England, but Obi advised him against it because Florence might resent it someday.
- Obi tells Christopher about Elsie Mark, who offered to have sex with him if he could get her an interview with the Board for a scholarship to England. She got the scholarship, even though Obi didn't sleep with her.
- Christopher tells Obi that he's dense, insisting that sex isn't bribery.
- Obi says it's wrong to take advantage of a girl who just wants an education.
- But Christopher replies that Obi is being naïve; a girl who offers to have sex with somebody so she can continue her education is not an innocent little schoolgirl.
- Obi says that even though she probably slept with the other board members, she'll always remember that there was at least one man who had principles.
- No, Christopher says, she probably thought Obi was impotent.
- Then he defines bribery as "improper influence" and says that if you slept with the girl who is already getting to appear before the Board, there's no influence at all.
- Likewise, Christopher continues, if you accept money from somebody who already is getting the job, that's not bribery either, since the person is already getting the job.
- His final argument is that if you accept money, you make a man poorer; but sleeping with a girl doesn't take anything away from her, so what's the harm?
- They argue for a long time, but as soon as the argument is over, Obi can't help but think about his father and the letter.

Chapter 13

- Obi takes two weeks' local leave to visit home.
- The night before he goes, Clara starts to cry when they are in bed. Obi asks what's the matter, and Clara says that it would be better if they broke off the engagement.
- Obi is hurt but he simply thanks her for everything. He paces the room, but then realizes that if he had seen another person behave that way, he would have accused them of being too dramatic. So he goes back to bed and finally, Clara convinces him to talk about it.
- She says there are two reasons they should not marry. The first is his family. But then she doesn't remember the second reason.
- Obi says he knows the second reason: it's because she doesn't want to marry somebody

who manages his finances so badly that he has to borrow money to pay for his insurance. When she starts to cry, he pulls her towards him and kisses her passionately.
- She tells him he must first apologize for what he said. He apologizes and she says she forgives him.
- Clara then realizes what has just happened – Obi has tricked her so they are no longer broken up.
- Obi sets out the next morning, bright and early.
- He decides to only spend one week at home, because of money. All the people in his village will expect him to share in his good fortune, and he simply can't afford it.
- Although he was given 24 pounds for his vacation, plus he has some left form his January salary, he knows he needs to pay for John's school fees while he has the money. Those cost 16 pounds, ten shillings.
- Obi's mother, Hannah, had just recently returned from the hospital. She's in her room.
- The narrator takes a moment to describe the difference between Hannah's room and Isaac's room.
- Due to his respect for the white man's culture and symbols, Isaac's room is full of the written word: books, papers, Scripture Union Cards. Hannah's room is full of clothes, pots of palm oil to make soap, last year's coco yams, kola nuts, and palm-ash.
- Obi starts to cry when he sees his mother in her bed. But she tells him that now she is healthy, compared to when she was ill.
- Later, some young women in the village who were passing by heard that Obi had returned, so they came inside and sang for him. This offended Isaac because it was heathen music, but Hannah liked it.

Chapter 14

- During evening prayers, Isaac prays against the devil and his works. Obi is pretty sure Clara is included in that.
- After prayers, Obi sits down with his father for a serious talk.
- Obi soon realizes that his father's strategy had included giving in to the girls singing heathen songs the night before, so that Obi's guard was down.
- Obi can see that his father is getting old when his hands shake as he pours the kerosene in the lantern. But it is also clear that his father still sees Obi as a child and that Obi still sees himself as a child: Obi doesn't offer to do it for him, knowing his father would never let children pour kerosene into a lamp.
- His father asks how their fellow villagers in Lagos are doing, and Obi admits that he hasn't seen them in a while, despite the regular Union meetings.
- His father chides him lightly, indicating that it is important to be with one's brothers when away from home.
- Then Isaac asks about Obi's girl.
- Obi says that he has no money but he wants to go meet her people and start negotiations for marriage.
- Then Isaac asks if they know where this girl comes from and Obi says yes, she is the daughter of Okeke from Mbaino.

- Isaac says it is surely not the retired teacher and Obi confirms that it is, indeed.
- Isaac laughs. He says a lot in that laugh – it is the kind of laugh that an ancestral spirit might laugh when talking with a lowly human who needs to be put in his place. Then Isaac tells Obi that he can't marry Clara because she is *osu*.
- Obi says he didn't think that mattered, since the Okonkwos are Christians.
- They argue.
- Isaac says they cannot go against this tradition, and Obi uses all the biblical arguments against isolating members of society. Obi argues that Christ had abolished these sorts of social and class distinctions, and that this kind of discrimination belongs to the old ways and the old religion.
- But Isaac will have none of it.
- He responds by saying that even great men in the Bible could be lepers. *Osus* are lepers in Igbo society. If Obi marries this girl, he will bring the shame of leprosy, not only into his own house, but also to his children and his grandchildren.
- Obi argues that this will change in time.
- Obi doesn't sleep that night, playing the argument over in his head. He knows he hasn't won –but he knows his father hasn't won either.
- And he's happy, not because of the argument but because he feels like he had a real conversation with his father for the first time in his 26 years.
- In the morning, he talks with his mother Hannah.
- Hannah tells him she had a dream one night. In the dream, she is sleeping in bed and wakes up to realize that termites had eaten the bed up from under her. She wondered what the dream meant. That same day, they received a letter from Joseph, telling them that Obi was going to marry an *osu*.
- At that moment, she knew what the dream meant. Then she tells Obi that if he is going to marry Clara, to wait until she is dead. If he does not wait, she will kill herself.
- Obi stays in his room that day. He does not even see the visitors who come to bring him wishes and greetings; they go away, offended.
- He does not go to evening prayers.
- His father comes in. Obi is lying on the bed and he waits to hear Isaac speak. He realizes that he wants another fight with his father, so he can beat him.
- But Obi also realizes that he has nothing real or good or honest to use as weapons to challenge his parents in this matter.
- Isaac is silent, so Obi finally tells him that he is returning to Lagos in two days.
- Isaac tells him that he was just a kid when he left his father's house to become a Christian. His father put a curse on him. He says that is a terrible thing to do to a child. Then his father killed himself and Isaac refused to go to the funeral. He says he gave up everything to become a Christian, so he knows more about Christianity than Obi can ever understand.
- Obi thinks about his grandfather and reflects on a particular story.
- His grandfather had killed Ikemefuna, a boy that had been given in exchange for the life of a woman who had been murdered. His grandfather had raised Ikemefuna as a son for some years before he killed him. Everybody knew it was a terrible thing to do, to kill a boy who called you father.

Chapter 15

- Obi is almost killed in an accident on the way back to Lagos. There is no damage to his car.
- He decides to stop at Clara's flat on the way to tell her, rather than going home first.
- But then he passes through the place where she lives, and goes home to take a bath. He's tired.
- He decides to visit Christopher, to get his advice. But finally, he just goes to Clara's.
- Obi tries to put on a good face.
- He says that it will all work out in the end. His mother is adamant but she will soon come around; his father can be convinced. They just need to lay low for a while until things calm down.
- Clara asks him if he's finished.
- Then she says there is only one thing she regrets, but it doesn't matter because she'll take care of it. She gives him her engagement ring back.
- He refuses to take it, so she threatens to throw it out the window. He tells her to go ahead. Then she takes the ring and drops it in his glove box.
- Obi wants to talk but Clara say no. Finally, after he sits there for ten minutes, she tells him to leave.
- Again, as he leaves, she says there was something she should have told him, but she would rather find another way to take care of it.
- Later, Christopher fails to be sympathetic. He said he had wanted to tell Obi not to be foolish but it's better not to interfere with these things when a man has his heart set on a particular woman.
- He laughs when Obi says that his mother threatened suicide, and tells a story about a woman who intended to do the same after her children died, but couldn't follow through with it.
- Obi says his mother very much meant what she said.
- Then he says he thinks Clara is pregnant.
- Christopher says he will find a doctor who can help Clara and Obi take care of it.
- The doctor they find, however, changes his mind when he sees Obi. He says he could go to jail and lose his license. He suggests that Obi marry Clara instead.
- Clara says she doesn't want to marry Obi.
- So they go to the next doctor. He doesn't like the idea but he'll do it for thirty pounds, cash.
- Obi asks if he won't take less money but he says no, since an abortion is a crime. He tells them to come back at two tomorrow, and reminds Clara not to eat.
- Then he asks Obi why he doesn't marry Clara. They don't answer.

Chapter 16

- Obi wonders how to find thirty pounds. He knows he still owes Clara fifty pounds but that can wait.
- He had only twelve pounds left from his home visit. He knows he can't ask Christopher,

who spends everything he earns almost immediately. Finally, he decides to ask the Hon. Sam Okoli, but he won't tell him what it's for, for Clara's sake.

- Then he remembers he should have stressed the need for secrecy to Christopher. But Christopher tells him you can't keep that kind of thing secret.
- The next day, the doctor counts the money carefully and tells Obi to return at 5pm.
- In the car, Obi can't drive away. He keeps thinking of all the bad things that could happen. He thinks he's not going to see Clara again.
- The doctor and Clara emerge from the office. Clara looks at him, then looks away.
- Obi thinks about shouting at her to stop, that they could go get married. But he does nothing.
- Obi decides to chase after the doctor's car but the car is already gone. He drives around this way and that way, looking for it, but no luck.
- At 5pm he returns to the clinic, but the doctor is still gone.
- He waits for an hour and a half. The doctor returns, without Clara. He tells Obi she's alright but he wants to watch her for the night just in case.
- Obi wants to see her. The doctor says he can see her in the morning, if she wants to, but she might not want to see him. Women are odd about things like this, he says.
- Obi tells his servant that he doesn't want dinner. Instead, he pulls out A.E. Housman's poems again, and finds the poem he wrote about Nigeria.
- He crumples it up and throws it away.
- In the morning, he tries to see the doctor again. The other patients grumble. Why would he be allowed to see a doctor, when he isn't even sick and doesn't have an appointment?
- Finally, he rushes inside, elbowing his way past the attendant who tries to prevent him from entering the clinic.
- The doctor lets him know that Clara is in the hospital, due to complications. But she'll be fine, he says.
- The patients are grumbling again when he comes out. One of them asks him whether he thinks he can do whatever he wants, just because he has a big car?
- At the hospital, Obi learns that Clara is too ill for visitors.

Chapter 17

- Mr. Green asks Obi if he had a good vacation. Then he tells Obi that he thinks it's shameful for Africans like Obi to ask for time off to go visit their homes when they have too many privileges as it is.
- Obi says that he doesn't care, but it is up to the Government.
- Mr. Green replies that it is people like Obi that ought to make the Government decide, but no African is willing to give up privileges even if it's in the best interest of the nation. Then he makes a snide remark about Nigerians' wish for democracy and self-governance.
- When Mr. Green leaves, Marie remarks that Mr. Green is speaking the truth – not about Obi, of course, but about a lot of Africans.
- Obi says that the Europeans were the ones who created all the "soft conditions" that Nigerians are now taking advantage of, so the British should stop blaming Africans for enjoying those privileges now.

- Marie tells him he looks ill. She advises him to go see a doctor.
- Obi goes to ask for a salary advance later that morning.
- Mr. Omo says it's possible but the way he says it indicates that it's really whether he wants to do it or not. Then he tells Obi that he needs a statement of expenditure to show how he spent the 25 pounds for his local leave; he must refund the balance.
- Obi realizes that the money given to him for his vacation was not a free gift. He does the math and discovers that he's only allowed 15 pounds. He can't refund the 10 pounds now.
- Now he realizes that he must analyze all his finances. He decides that the 20 pounds he must give every month to the Umuofia Progressive Union is the factor that has contributed to or caused all his problems.
- He decides not to pay it anymore until he can see an end to his financial nightmare. If they ask why, he'll tell them he has some family commitments he has to attend to first. They won't take him to court – he's family.
- A messenger returns with a letter.
- He had decided to write to Clara the night before and she has returned the letter, unopened. He had realized that he had no right to be angry, or at least, Clara had more right to be angry than he did.
- So he had written a letter saying he understood if she never wanted to see him again but he hoped she would give him another chance. He had taken the letter to the hospital, leaving it with a nurse.

Chapter 18

- Clara is in the hospital for five weeks. She is given 70 days' leave so she leaves Lagos.
- Christopher advises Obi to wait before trying to see her; if Obi gives Clara time she will come back to him.
- Obi had planned to pay back the fifty pounds he owed her, but then he received his income tax bill. 32 pounds. Marie advises him to pay monthly installments.
- Then Hannah Okonkwo dies. He sends as much money as he can, but the people of Umuofia say she should have had a better funeral, given that her son has a European post. It was shameful, one attendee told the Umuofia Progressive Union. It was clear Obi spent all his time and money on fast living.
- Then they discuss how he never comes to the Union meetings anymore, that he seems to have abandoned his family and kinsmen (i.e., his friends and fellow citizens from Umuofia.) They discuss how the apple seems not to have fallen far from the tree: Isaac Okonkwo did the same thing, abandoning his own father for Christianity.
- Obi is stricken with grief at the news of his mother's death. Mr. Green gives him a week's leave, but Obi only takes two days. He doesn't even go to Umuofia, knowing she would already have been buried by the time he arrives.
- But at home, when he is alone, he cries and cries. Then he sleeps without waking, something he could not remember happening to him for many years.
- He wakes up and feels shame and guilt again. He thinks about how alone his father will be without his mother.

- As he begins his daily ablutions, he accidentally brushes his teeth with shaving cream.
- Joseph arrives in a taxi. He brings a dozen bottles of beer.
- Obi is wondering why, but soon Umuofia's expatriates appear to bring their greetings to Obi and show honor to his mother. Over 25 men come to be with Obi.
- They use the beer to entertain. Joseph says Obi should use eight bottles today, and save the rest for those who will come tomorrow.
- The mourners gossip and talk, and in silence, everybody hears one of the mourners, Nathaniel, telling a story about Tortoise who told his people not to send for him unless there was something new that happened. When his mother died, the people wondered how they could get him to return for her funeral, so they told him that his father's palm tree had miraculously sprouted fruit form the end of its leaf. He went home to see it and ended up attending his mother's funeral.
- Everybody, including Obi, hears the tale. They are silent, and embarrassed.
- Obi sleeps that night and feels guilty again in the morning when he wakes up. But the ache he feels is beginning to leave. In fact, he feels calm. Peace even.
- He eats a lot, and remembers how King David in the Bible refused to eat when his son was sick but as soon as he heard his son was dead, he got up and ate. He also must have felt peaceful in the wake of grief.

Chapter 19

- Obi feels a sense of renewed vitality, a sense of rebirth, after the guilt over his mother's death is gone.
- He starts to remember his mother as a woman who got things done, as the woman who ruled the household (rather than Obi's father).
- His favorite story to remember is the one where the priest of Udo's goat wanders into his mother's kitchen and his mother, angry at how often the goat had wandered into their yard and disturbed Isaac's shrine, sawed off its head.
- Though the village was angry with her, eventually they calmed down. Why? Because she was a Christian, part of the white man's religion, and its god had clearly trumped the village's god.
- It's now the time again to choose who would be the recipient of the scholarship. One day, a businessman comes to visit Obi at home. He tells Obi that his son is going to England in September and needs the scholarship. He offers Obi 50 pounds.
- Obi told him now, that all he does is make recommendations to the Board – he doesn't choose the recipient.
- That's OK, the man says. That's perfect.
- Obi knows the man's son is already on the short list. He'll already appear before the board. He asks the man why he doesn't pay for his son; the scholarship should go to those who are less fortunate. The man laughs and says there is never enough money in the world.
- He drops the 50 pounds on the table.
- When he goes, Obi covers the money with his newspaper. He is ashamed. He has trouble sleeping that night.

* He takes one of the scholarship applicants dancing. Then he takes her to bed.
* She is also on the short list. But she seems to know what to do.
* There were others, more bribes. But he does have a code of ethics; he won't take bribes from those who don't meet the minimum qualifications.
* With all the help from the bribes, Obi is able to pay off his debts.
* One day, a man leaves 20 pounds and Obi thinks, *Enough is enough*.
* But it's too late. A knock on the door. It's the police.
* We have now come full circle, back to the beginning.
* Everybody wonders why Obi did it, and how he became corrupt. The judge, the British Council men, the men who belonged to the Umuofia Progressive Union – none of them knows why. Even Mr. Green really had no idea.

Themes

Theme of Identity

Obi's identity is shaped by two dual forces: Western culture and values and Igbo culture and values. Though Obi embraces Western values as evidenced through his education and his nominal adherence to Christianity, we can see how this decision alienates him from his traditional Igbo culture. For Obi to identify with Western culture means that he rejects a number of cultural traditions including polygamy, paying a bride-price (misunderstood by the British as "buying a wife"), honoring a man because of his many "titles" earned through competitions, religious observance, etc. Embracing Western culture means embracing the many positive and negative things that came with the industrial revolution and other defining moments of Western history.

Obi sees himself as a pioneer. He wants to change the corrupt system of bribery and nepotism, and he wants to marry a girl that traditionally is taboo. We can see how much this identity meant to him when he cries after the judge asks how a man of such "education" and "promise" could have accepted bribes. He has failed. And now that too is part of his identity.

Questions About Identity

1. How is Obi's identity shaped by his family? By his religion? By his education? By his job?
2. In what way do these factors that shape Obi's identity lead to alienation and isolation?
3. If Obi defines his position in society in one way, how do his family and friends define his position in society? How does that obligate him in ways he feels are inconsistent with his identity as an individual?
4. In what way is Obi's identity linked to his social, cultural, and financial duties?

Chew on Identity

Although Obi sees himself as an individual, his kinsmen maintain a group identity and incorporate Obi into their system of socialism and nepotism, creating a web of obligations and expectations that Obi finds difficult to escape.

Obi identifies himself as an educated Igbo, believing that he is as fully Igbo as he is educated; but in reality, his education has isolated and alienated him from his indigenous culture.

Theme of Duty

Obi's downfall is related to the many expensive duties he suddenly acquired after he returned home from England. Suddenly, he was responsible for providing for his parents' retirement income, paying his brother's school fees, repaying the Umuofia Progressive Union for the scholarship that allowed him to get his college education, and, last but not least, keeping up the social appearances and obligations of a man of his position. This last duty involves buying and maintaining a car, keeping a "boy" to cook and shop for him, and dressing appropriately for social functions.

Questions About Duty

1. What are Obi's financial, cultural, and moral obligations?
2. Why do all these obligations come into conflict?
3. Where there ways for Obi to fulfill his obligations, while maintaining his self-respect, principles, and an individual identity? Why or why not?

Chew on Duty

Although Obi sees himself as an individual, his kinsmen maintain a group identity and incorporate Obi into their system of socialism and nepotism, creating a web of obligations and expectations that Obi finds difficult to escape.

Although Obi believes that his duties become his financial ruin, in reality it is his own poor financial planning that causes his downfall.

Theme of Lies and Deceit

According to *No Longer At Ease*, corruption is an integral part of the Nigerian civil and business system. In order to get a job or a scholarship, bribery seems to be a necessary step. Obi, a young man educated in Great Britain, believes strongly that education is the key to ending corruption. Ultimately, though, he too succumbs to temptation when he discovers that his salary is insufficient to meet all his financial obligations.

Questions About Lies and Deceit

1. What lies does Obi tell himself? What lies does he tell his family, his friends? What lies does he tell Clara?

2. Why does Obi find himself lying so much? Does he deceive anybody? Does he deceive himself? Why or why not?
3. What other characters in the book are deceptive?
4. Do you agree with Obi's belief that education is the best way to fight corruption?

Chew on Lies and Deceit

Although Obi falls victim to corruption and bribery, it is not because he is inherently corruptible; rather, he is vulnerable because he spent so much time lying to the people he loves.

Even though Obi is correct that education may be a corrective force for corruption, he fails to account for how hubris and self-righteousness can lead to one's downfall.

Theme of Society and Class

Education is critical for social position and status in Nigeria, as presented by *No Longer At Ease* . With an education, your salary jumps to five times the amount you might obtain without an education. In *No Longer At Ease* Obi discovers that being a part of the educated elite, however, is a double-edged sword. On the one hand, it provides him with privileges, wealth, and admiration. But he soon discovers that it is impossible to maintain the lifestyle expected of him as a senior civil servant while fulfilling his duties to his parents and to the Umuofia Progressive Union. The more money he spends to maintain his lifestyle, the more money he needs.

Questions About Society and Class

1. What does it take to get into the "elite" class in Nigerian society?
2. What does it take to *stay* in the elite class in Nigerian society?
3. Is it possible to argue that Obi's desire to maintain a lavish, luxurious lifestyle is the root of all his problems?

Chew on Society and Class

Although education proved to be the ticket to entering elite society, intelligence and education could not keep Obi there; only financial stability could enable Obi to keep his elite position.

Even though the Umuofia Progressive Union helped Obi achieve his social status by providing the money for his education, they were unable to help him keep his position because they did not understand how expensive it was for Obi to maintain his social status once he entered the ranks of the elite.

Theme of Family

In Igbo culture, family has a broad definition. Not only are Obi's parents and siblings his family, but all the men and women who come from his region are also considered his kinsmen. While on the one hand this means that Obi has a strong social network and support system, it also means that his web of obligations is broad. Obi ultimately finds his duties as a member of the Umuofia and as a member of his own family to be burdensome.

Questions About Family

1. How does Obi define family? How do his friends and family members define it?
2. Why do African societies have a broader definition of family than is found in Western cultures?
3. What advantages are there to having a broader definition of family? What disadvantages are there?
4. Is the African definition of family similar to the concept of "socialism" or can you find distinguishing characteristics between the two systems?

Chew on Family

Because Obi has absorbed the western notion of the nuclear family, and because he feels contempt for much of his indigenous culture, he fails to recognize the Umuofia Progressive Union as an extended support system for him during his time of need.

Although Obi is willing to flout custom when it offends only his friends in Lagos, he is unwilling to choose Clara over his family, especially when he realizes how isolated he will be if he does so.

Theme of Marriage

Obi Okonkwo has absorbed Western ideals of marriage, believing that he should be allowed to marry whomever he wants, whenever he wants, because it only affects himself. But when he falls in love with a woman of an "untouchable" caste, and his family and friends are not ready for a revolution in marriage traditions, Obi discovers that he is unwilling to be a pioneer if it means rejection and isolation. Ultimately, he acquiesces to the wishes of his friends and family.

Questions About Marriage

1. What is the difference between marriage customs in western society and marriage customs in Igbo society?
2. What is the bride-price? Why is it important in Igbo society?
3. Why doesn't Obi want to pay a bride-price when he gets married? Are his reasons convincing, or is it simply another example of how he is alienated from his own culture?
4. Why is it forbidden to marry Clara in Igbo culture? Do you think it's acceptable for some people to be considered non-marriageable in society? Do we have any examples of this in Western society?

Chew on Marriage

Although Obi believes the time has come to accept Western norms for marriage, he discovers that certain traditions – like class and social status – are stronger than he realized.

Even though Obi believes that his love for Clara is stronger than his need to be accepted by society, and even though he sees himself as an individual, he soon realizes that he personally is incapable of defying his family's wishes.

Theme of Dreams, Hopes, Plans

All characters in *No Longer At Ease* has dreams and hopes that they want to fulfill. Unfortunately, these hopes and dreams often conflict with the reality of their life situations. Obi Okonkwo wants to be part of the elite, but he hopes to do so without succumbing to corruption. He also wants to marry Clara, even though Igbo culture forbids him to do so. Isaac and Hannah Okonkwo want to see their son be a good Christian and to use the power of the written word to succeed, but they cannot let go of the part of their culture that forbids marriage to an *osu*. Ultimately, Obi's family and kinsmen prevent his marriage to Clara, and he succumbs to the temptation of accepting bribes. Obi's dreams, hopes, and plans fail completely.

Questions About Dreams, Hopes, Plans

1. What are Obi's dreams, hopes, and plans? What are Clara's? What about Isaac and Hannah?
2. What prevents all these characters from achieving their dreams? Is it possible to blame the colonial situation? The clash between cultures? Religion? Personal character flaws?

Chew on Dreams, Hopes, Plans

Although Obi believes it is his backward Igbo culture that prevents him from getting what he wants, it is actually his personal character flaws that get in the way.

Although Obi discovers a lot of obstacles for achieving his dreams, ultimately it is simply his lack of foresight that causes his difficulties.

Theme of Love

Although Obi does love Clara, he has allowed his infatuation with her to blind him to the reality of their situation. Ultimately, *No Longer At Ease* appears to suggest that love is not a weapon that can defend two individuals against disapproval, social stigma, or cultural customs. Love fails to be stronger than cultural and familial expectations.

Questions About Love

1. Is love always the same, or do different cultures define it differently? If you believe it's always the same, why? What similarities do you see between a typical love affair in the U.S. and Clara and Obi's love affair?

2. If you believe that love is defined differently in different cultures, what differences do you see in this book?
3. What role does love play in marriage, according to the ideas expressed in this book?
4. Do you believe love should trump or transcend all taboos on marriage? Why or why not?

Chew on Love

Although Obi loves Clara, his love for her fails to be stronger than the familial and cultural obstacles they encounter.

Obi thinks he loves Clara, but he just loves the idea of her; when faced with the reality of what it would mean to forsake his friends and family for her, he is unable to remain committed. Clara, alternatively, remains faithful even when she sees Obi unraveling financially.

Theme of Principles

Obi absorbed Western values and customs during his time in England. These values extended from the belief that he should be able to choose his own wife to the belief that education was a cure for corruption. Although Western values and culture had been destructive to Igbo culture at times, *No Longer At Ease* seems to suggest that the collective energy of Igbo values and traditions has the power to defeat newly-acquired Western values.

Questions About Principles

1. What are Obi's principles at the start of the book, before his trial? What are his principles by the end of the book?
2. Compare and contrast Obi's principles with the principles he despises – the system of bribery, and nepotism he encounters in Nigerian politics.
3. Compare and contrast Obi's principles with those of Joseph, Clara, and his family.
4. Why was Obi unable to adhere to his own principles?

Chew on Principles

The problem with Obi's principles are that they are too rigid; he doesn't recognize value in the indigenous system. Instead, he turns to the cold value system of the colonizer, which offers him little in the way of a support system.

Although *No Longer At Ease* seems to condemn the system of bribery and corruption that exists within modern Nigeria, we also see that there are clear advantages to it: that system belongs to a more positive system of socialism and collective welfare, with all parties mutually benefiting from their many relationships.

Theme of Isolation

Obi left Nigeria for college in England at the typical age. Isolated and alone in a foreign country, he fell in love with his native land. He longed for it in that nostalgic, homesick way that caused him to paint an idealistic picture in his head, which bore little resemblance to reality. When he returns to Nigeria, he's not quite prepared for the reality he faces. He is forced to confront corruption that exists in every segment of society, while combating certain social customs that are socially restrictive, like restrictions on marriage. These cultural values are still entrenched in Nigerian society despite the introduction of Western values and Christianity. As a result, Obi finds himself increasingly isolated and alienated from his friends and family and, ultimately, his lover.

Questions About Isolation

1. How does homesickness shape Obi's perception of Nigeria? Of his family?
2. How does Christianity serve to be an isolating factor for the Okonkwo family? In what way does it fail to isolate them?
3. What role does education play in isolating and alienating Obi from his friends, family, and culture?
4. Was it inevitable for Obi to become alienated because of his education in England?

Chew on Isolation

Although Obi's western education alienated him from his friends and family and gave him a new set of values, it could not prevent him from falling back into the corrupt system at home.

Although Obi displays classic symptoms of what has been called the "postcolonial identity," it would be insufficient to blame his downfall simply on his alienation from his mother culture and tongue.

Quotes

Identity Quotes

Obi's listlessness did not show any signs of decreasing even when the judge began to sum up. It was only when he said: "I cannot comprehend how a young man of your education and brilliant promise could have done this" that a sudden and marked change occurred. Treacherous tears came into Obi's eyes....All that stuff about education and promise and betrayal had not taken him unawares....

In fact, some weeks ago when the trial first began, Mr. Green, his boss, who was one of the Crown witnesses, had also said something about a young man of great promise. And Obi had remained completely unmoved....But now when the supreme moment came he was betrayed by treacherous tears. (1.9-10)

Thought: Obi had always been principled. He believed that his education made him less prone to corruption because he was able to advance in his career without bribery. But now, faced with his own deceit, he has to admit that his identity as a "young man" of such "brilliant promise" is forever cheapened. For more on Obi's downfall, check on his "Character Analysis."

Joseph was not very happy when Obi told him the story of the interview. His opinion was that a man in need of a job could not afford to be angry.

"Nonsense!" said Obi. "That's what I call colonial mentality."

"Call it what you like," said Joseph in Igbo. "You know more book than I, but I am older and wiser. And I can tell you that a man does not challenge his chi to a wrestling match. (5. 16-18)

Thought: Joseph here is telling Obi the equivalent of the English saying, "Pride goeth before a fall." Obi's hubris – his assumption that *he* cannot be corrupted because he is educated and understands more than the common man on the street – will be his downfall.

"We have our faults, but we are not empty men who become white when they see white, and black when they see black."

Obi's heart glowed with pride with in him.

"He is the grandson of Ogbuefi Okonkwo who faced the white man single-handed and died in the fight. Stand up!"

Obi stood up obediently.

"Remark him," said Odogwu. "He is Ogbuefi Okonkwo come back. He is Okonkwo kpom-kwem, exact, perfect." (5.100-104)

Thought: The men of Umuofia begin to bestow an identity on Obi. They suggest he is his grandfather reincarnated, and that means part of his job will be to stand proud as a black man, and to stand up to the white man.

She [Hannah] was a very devout woman, but Obi used to wonder whether, left to herself, she would not have preferred telling her children the folk stories that her mother had told her. In fact, she used to tell her eldest daughters stories. But that was before Obi was born. She stopped because her husband forbade her to do so.

"We are not heathens," he had said. "Stores like that are not for the people of the Church."

And Hannah had stopped telling her children folk stories. She was loyal to her husband and to her new faith. Her mother had joined the Church with her children after her husband's death. Hannah had already grown up when they ceased to be "people of nothing" and joined the "people of the Church." Such was the confidence of the early Christians that they called the others "the people of nothing" or sometimes, when they felt more charitable, "the people of the world."

Isaac Okonkwo was not merely a Christian; he was a catechist. In their first years of married life he made Hannah see the grave responsibility she carried as a catechist's wife. (6.21-24)

Thought: Isaac and Hannah Okonkwo are part of the first generation of Africans to assume a new identity: they embrace Christianity as their religion and forsaking their cultural customs and beliefs. For Isaac, Christianity it is not just a word, but is an entire lifestyle. For Hannah, it is part of her identity as Isaac's wife. Check out Isaac's "Character Analysis" to get a better sense of his relationship to Christianity.

"I can't marry you," she said suddenly...

"I don't understand you, Clara." And he really didn't. Was this woman's game to bind him more firmly? But Clara was not like that; she had no coyness in her....

"Why can't you marry me?" He succeeded in sounding unruffled. For answer she threw herself at him and began to weep violently on his shoulder.

"What the matter, Clara? Tell me." He was no longer unruffled. There was a hint of tears in his voice.

"I am an osu," she wept. Silence. She stopped weeping and quietly disengaged herself form him. Still he said nothing.

"So you see we cannot get married," she said, quite firmly, almost gaily—a terrible kind of gaiety. Only the tears showed she had wept.

"Nonsense!" said Obi. He shouted it almost, as if by shouting it now he could wipe away those seconds of silence, when everything had seemed to stop, waiting in vain for him to speak. (7.58-64)

Thought: In the first of many scenes where Clara tells Obi she cannot marry him, she admits her identity as part of a forbidden caste. And though Obi is quick to say that it doesn't matter, the few seconds of silence indicate that it really *does* matter. If he marries Clara, his own identity will forever be linked to that of an untouchable class.

"I was thinking how such a good and beautiful girl could remain unmarried until now." (7.66)

Thought: When Joseph hears that Clara is an *osu*, his response is similar to that of women who wonder what's wrong with an incredible guy they meet. They wonder why he wasn't snatched up before, but soon discover that he's married.

"Look at me," said Joseph..."You know book, but this is no matter for book. Do you know what an osu is? But how can you know?" In that short question he said in effect that Obi's mission-house upbringing and European education had made him a stranger in his country—the most painful thing one could say to Obi.

I know more about it than yourself," he said, "and I'm going to marry the girl. I wasn't actually seeking your approval." (7.70-71)

Thought: Obi is smart, and educated in a British university. His parents are Christians who forsook many aspects of Igbo culture to embrace a Western religion. Joseph's doubt that Obi understands what he's doing by planning to marry an *osu* indicates a fundamental doubt in Obi's African-ness. But Obi responds with anger and justification: his declaration indicates that he believes he is just as African, perhaps more so, than Joseph himself. This passage is one of several that hint at Obi's "postcolonial" identity. Not only was he educated in Western institutions, but his unwillingness to adhere to African customs puts his identity as a true-blue Igbo man in doubt.

Mother's room was the most distinctive in the whole house, except perhaps for Father's....Mr. Okonkwo believed utterly and completely in the things of the white man. And the symbol of the white man's power was the written word, or better still, the printed word.... The result of Okonkwo's mystic regard for the written word was that his room was full of old books and papers—from Blackie's Arithmetic, which he used in 1908, to Obi's Durell, from obsolete cockroach-eaten translations of the Bible into the Onitsha dialect to yellowed Scripture Union Cards of 1920 and earlier. Okonkwo never destroyed a piece of paper. He had two boxes full of them. The rest were preserved on top of his enormous cupboard, on tables, on boxes and on one corner of the floor. (13.24; 27)

Thought: Isaac Okonkwo's identification with the things of the white man is evident here; his identity is wrapped up with the power of the white man, and that of the written word. We talk more about what "the written word" symbolizes in "Symbols, Imagery, Allegory."

"I was no more than a boy when I left my father's house and went with the missionaries. He placed a curse on me. I as not there but my brothers told me it was true. When a man curses his own child it is a terrible thing. And I was his first son."

Obi had never heard about the curse....

"When they brought me word that he had hanged himself I told them that those who live by the sword must perish by the sword. Mr. Braddeley, the white man who was our teacher, said it was not the right thing to say and told me to go home for the burial. I refused to go. Mr. Braddeley thought I spoke about the white man's messenger whom my father killed. He did not know I spoke about Ikemefuna, with whom I grew up in my mother's hut until the day came when my father killed him with his own hands." He paused to collect his thoughts, turned in his chair, and faced the bed on which Obi lay. "I tell you all this so that you may know what it was in those days to become a Christian. I left my father's house, and he placed a curse on me. I went

through fire to become a Christian. Because I suffered I understand Christianity—more than you will ever do." (14.58-60)

Thought: Obi tries to convince his father that, as a Christian, he should not mind that Obi would marry an *osu*. Isaac asserts his Christian identity by claiming that he gave up everything in order to become a Christian: family, privilege, friends. In this passage, Isaac suggests that Obi does not know what that is like, and has no right to try to use Biblical arguments against his father.

Everybody wondered why. The learned judge, as we have seen, could not comprehend how an educated young man and so on and so forth. The British Council man, even the men of Umuofia, did not know. And we must presume that, in spite of his certitude, Mr. Green did not know either. (19.29)

Thought: In the end, Obi's reputation is forever tarnished. His identity as an educated young man who didn't need to take bribes has been taken away from him. The part of his identity that he didn't take seriously was his ego. Obi had the classic tragic flaw, hubris (excessive pride). His pride made him blind to all the other flaws in his character that made him vulnerable to accepting bribes in the end. Be sure to read up on "Genre" and "Character Clues" to get a more complete sense of how Obi fell to such depths.

Duty Quotes

Everybody was properly dressed in aghada or European suit except the guest of honor, who appeared in his shirtsleeves because of the heat. That was Obi's mistake Number One. Everybody expected a young man from England to be impressively turned out. (4.11)

Thought: It is Obi's duty, as the educated son of Umuofia, to appear decently clothed and to fulfill his social and financial obligations to the Umuofia Progressive Union. This is especially true of his reception, which included members of the press.

"Our people have a saying 'Ours is ours, but mine is mine.' Every village struggles at this momentous epoch in our political evolution to possess that of which it can say: 'This is mine.' We are happy that today we have such an invaluable possession in the person of our illustrious son and guest of honor."

He traced the history of the Umuofia Scholarship Scheme, which had made it possible for Obi to study overseas, and called it an investment which must yield heavy dividends. He then referred (quite obliquely, of course) to the arrangement whereby the beneficiary from this scheme as expected to repay his debt over four years so that "an endless stream of students will be enabled to drink deep at the Pierian Spring of knowledge." (4.16-17)

Thought: Obi's duty goes beyond repaying his scholarship. He also represents the village's investment in the future. His duty is to be an example, to provide the education of other Umuofian young people, to represent the village in government, and to lift the Umuofia out of poverty.

Four years in England had filled Obi with a longing to be back in Umuofia. The feeling was sometimes so strong that he found himself feeling ashamed of studying English for his degree. He spoke Igbo whenever he had the least opportunity of doing so. Nothing gave him greater pleasure than to find another Igbo-speaking student in a London bus. But when he had to speak in English with a Nigerian student from another tribe he lowered his voice. It was humiliating to have to speak to one's countryman in a foreign language, especially in the presence of the proud owners of that language. They would naturally assume that one had no language of one's own. He wished they were here today to see. Let them come to Umuofia now and listen to the talk of men who made a great art of conversation. Let them come and see men and women and children who knew how to live, whose joy of life had not yet been killed by those who claimed to teach other nations how to live. (5.73)

Thought: Alone in England, Obi felt the sting of the British assumption that they are superior to the colonized African peoples. He felt bereft of his culture and denied his language, especially when he had to speak the language of the colonizer with other Africans abroad. Now in his hometown, he is proud to realize that Africans have not yet taken on the habit of self-deprecation, a symptom of being colonized.

Obi did not sleep for a long time after he had lain down. He thought about his responsibilities. It was clear that his parents could no longer stand on their own….

"I must give them a monthly allowance from my salary." How much? Could he afford ten pounds? If only he did not have to pay back twenty pounds a month to the Umuofia Progressive Union. Then there was John's school fees.

"We'll manage somehow," he said aloud to himself. "One cannot have it both ways. There are many young man in this country today who would sacrifice themselves to get the opportunity I have had." (6. 37-39)

Thought: Obi feels his duty as a son deeply. Although it will come at a significant cost, he does what he can to help his parents financially. Before he even begins to pay back his college scholarship to the Umuofia Progressive Union, he resents that he is indebted to this organization.

"What is a pioneer? Someone who shows the way. That is what I am doing. Anyway it is too late to change now."

"It is not," said Joseph. "What is an engagement ring? Our fathers did not marry with rings. It is not too late to change. Remember you are the one and only Umuofia son to be educated overseas. We do not want to be like the unfortunate child who grows his first tooth and grows a decayed one. What sort of encouragement will your action give to the poor men and women who collected the money?"

Obi was getting a little angry. "It was only a loan, remember. I shall pay it all back to the last anini." (7.105-107)

Thought: Joseph reminds Obi that his duty, as the first college-educated son of Umuofia, is to show the way and break the path for others. That means being a pioneer, but it does not mean flaunting customs and breaking the taboos of their people. Instead, he should be a model of respectability.

"Let joking pass," said the old man who had earlier on greeted Umuofia in a warlike salute. "Joshua is now without a job. We have given him ten pounds. But ten pounds does not talk. If you stand a hundred pounds here where I stand now, it will not talk. That is why we say that he who has people is richer than he who has money. Everyone of us here should look out for openings in his department and put in a word for Joshua. This was greeted with approval.

"Thanks to the Man Above," he continued, "we now have one of our sons in the senior service. We are not going to ask him to bring his salary to share among us. It is in little things like this that he can help us. It is our fault if we do not approach him...."

"Your words are very good," said the President. "We have the same thought in our minds. But we must give the young man time to look round first and know what is what."

The meeting supported the President by their murmurs. "Give the young man time." "Let him settle down." Obi felt very uneasy. But he knew they meant well. Perhaps it would not be too difficult to manage them. (8.24-27)

Thought: As Obi sits in the Umuofia Progressive Union and hears the men talk about what they expect their "son" in the senior service to do for them. Obi realizes that his duties to his fellow kin will interfere with his principles not to take bribes or be corrupt.

"As you all know, it takes a little time to settle down again after an absence of four years. I have many little private matters to settle. My request is this, that you give me four months before I start to pay back my loan."

Yes, it was a small matter. But it was clear that not everyone thought so. Obi even heard someone ask what he was going to do with the big money which Government would give him....

"I know what Government pays senior service people. What you get in one month is what some of your brothers here get in one year. I have already said that we will give you four months. We can even give you one year. But are we doing you any good?"

A big lump caught in Obi's throat.

"What the Government pays you is more than enough unless you go into bad ways....You may ask why I am saying all this, I have heard that you are moving around with a girl of doubtful

ancestry, and even thinking o marrying her."

Obi leapt to his feet trembling with rage. (8.31-32; 37-40)

Thought: Obi wants to do his duty to his parents, and that makes his duty to pay back his scholarship difficult. Though he has no intention of dishonoring that duty, he asks for a respite until he gets on his feet, a break that some people do not want to grant him. The President of the Union reminds Obi that his monthly salary is larger than what many men in the room make in a year. He adds that Obi is perhaps having a hard time managing his money because of his association with a girl of questionable heritage. Obi gets angry and insists that he'll start paying the loan back instantly. Later, he regrets this decision when he runs into financial trouble.

And if one thought objectively of the matter...could one blame those poor men for being critical of a senior service man who appeared reluctant to pay twenty pounds a month? They had taxed themselves mercilessly to raise eighth hundred pounds to send him to England. Some of them earned no more than five pounds a month. He earned nearly fifty. They had wives and school going children; he had none. After paying the twenty pounds he would have thirty left. And very soon he would have an increment which alone was as big as some people's salary.

Obi admitted that his people had a sizable point. What they did not know was that, having labored in sweat and tears to enroll their kinsman among the shining elite, they had to keep him there. Having made him a member of an exclusive club whose members greet one another with "how's the car behaving?" did they expect him to turn round and answer: "I'm sorry, but my car is off the road. You see I couldn't pay my insurance premium"? That would be letting the side down in a way that was quite unthinkable. (10.16-17)

Thought: Obi realizes that if he has a duty to pay his kinsmen back for the scholarship money. The board has a duty to make sure he stays within the elite society.

Obi had long come to admit to himself that, no matter how much he disliked Mr. Green, he nevertheless had some admirable qualities. Take, for instance, his devotion to duty. Rain or shine, he was in the office half an hour before the official time, and quite often worked long after two, or returned again in the evening. Obi could not understand it. Here was a man who did not believe in a country, and yet worked so hard for it. Did he simply believe in duty as a logical necessity? (11.9)

Thought: Though Mr. Green may be the symbol of colonial hubris, he also represents the hard-working European who toils for his country, and for his country's colonial possessions, even though he has little to gain.

Obi had exactly thirty-four pounds, nine and three-pence when he set out. Twenty-five pounds was his local leave allowance, which was paid to all senior civil servants for no other reason than that they went on local leave. The rest was the remains of his January salary. With thirty-four pounds one might possibly last two weeks at home, although a man like Obi, with a car and a "European post," would normally be expected to do better. But sixteen pounds ten shillings was to go into brother John's school fees for the second term, which began in April. Obi knew that unless he paid the fees now that he had a lump sum in his pocket, he might not be able to do so when the time came. (13. 19)

Thought: Obi's position in society means he should be more generous with his kinsmen when he goes home to visit. His familial obligations and personal circumstances mean he's ultimately stingy and doesn't fully live up to expectations.

Lies and Deceit Quotes

"I cannot understand why he [Obi] did it," said the British Council man thoughtfully....

"I can," said Mr. Green simply. "What I can't understand is why people like you refuse to face facts." Mr. Green was famous for speaking his mind. He wiped his red face with the white towel on his neck. "The African is corrupt through and through....The fact that over countless centuries the African has been the victim of the worst climate in the world and of every imaginable disease. Hardly his fault. But he has been sapped mentally and physically. We have brought him Western education. But what use is it to him?" (1.12-13;16)

Thought: Mr. Green attributes the physical environment as the evolutionary catalyst for corruption in Africa – a blanket generalization, to say the least. He further generalizes and attributes the characteristic to all Africans, regardless of education. See Mr. Green's "Character Analysis" for more on his role in *No Longer At Ease*.

"It is all lack of experience," said another man. "He should not have accepted the money himself. What others do is tell you to go and hand it to their houseboy. Obi tried to do what everyone does without finding out how it as done." He told the proverb of the house rat who went swimming with his friend the lizard and died from cold, for while the lizard's scales kept him dry the rat's hairy body remained wet. (1.36)

Thought: The men at the Umuofia Progressive Union weren't concerned so much with the fact that Obi accepted bribes. Rather, they take issue with the fact that he accepted bribes without covering up his tracks. Because of such reckless behavior, it is inevitable that he would get caught.

"But take one of these old men. He probably left school thirty years ago in Standard Six. He has worked steadily to the top through bribery—an ordeal by bribery. To him the bribe is natural. He gave it and he expects it. Our people say that if you pay homage to the man on top, others will pay homage to you when it is your turn to be on top. Well, that is what the old men say."

"What do the young men say, if I may ask?"

"To most of them bribery is no problem. They come straight to eh top without bribing anyone.

It's not that they're necessarily better than others, it's simply that they can afford to be virtuous. But even that kind of virtue can become a habit." (2.31-33)

Thought: According to this passage, lies and deceit belong to uneducated men who lack opportunities. Virtue is a by-product of education, and ultimately, it creates an incorruptible soul.

"Of course those of you who know book will not have any difficulty," said the Vice-President on Obi's left. "Otherwise I would have suggested seeing some of the men beforehand."

"It would not be necessary," said the President, "since they would be mostly white men."

"You think white men don't eat bribe? Come to our department. They eat more than black men nowadays." (4.24-26)

Thought: After asking Obi whether he has a job yet or not, the men of Umuofia describe how widespread corruption is in the system. They claim that without an education, it is impossible to get a job without relying on corrupt tactics.

Obi's theory that the public service of Nigeria would remain corrupt until the old Africans at the top were replaced by young men from the universities was first formulated in a paper read to the Nigerian Students' Union in London. But unlike most theories formed by students in London, this one survived the first impact of homecoming. In fact, within a month of his return Obi came across two classic examples of his old African. (5.1)

Thought: Though Obi's theories on corruption within the Nigerian governmental system are initially confirmed, the novel seems to imply that it won't be long before his beliefs will be challenged.

"Why do you want a job in the civil service? So that you can take bribes?" he asked.

Obi hesitated. His first impulse was to say it was an idiotic question. He said instead: "I don't know how you expect me to answer that question. Even if my reason is to take bribes, you don't expect me to admit it before this board. So I don't think it's a very useful question."...

Joseph was not very happy when Obi told him the story of the interview. His opinion was that a man in need of a job could not afford to be angry.

"Nonsense!" said Obi. "That's what I call colonial mentality. (5. 13-14; 16-17)

Thought: To ignore the corruption in Nigeria is, for Obi, a function of the colonial system. According to his viewpoint, the colonial system created the corrupt system by rewarding obsequiousness, homage, patronage, and thus, by extension, bribery and deceit.

Throughout that morning Obi felt strangely elated. It was not unlike the feeling he had some years ago in England after his first woman...

After his encounter with Mr. Mark he did feel like a tiger. He had won his first battle hands-down. Everyone said it was impossible to win....It was easy to keep one's hands clean. It required no more than the ability to say: "I'm sorry, Mr. So-and-So, but I cannot continue this discussion. Good morning." One should not, of course, be unduly arrogant. After all, the temptation was not really overwhelming. But in all modesty one could not say it had been nonexistent. Obi was finding it more and more impossible to live on what was left of his forty-seven pounds ten after he had paid twenty to the Umuofia Progressive Union and sent ten to his parents. Even now he had no idea where John's school fees or next term would come from. No, one could not say he had no need of money. (9.41-42)

Thought: When the first opportunity to take a bribe comes, Obi finds it easy to say no. But it is the first time of many temptations to come, and Obi hasn't yet begun his downward slide into financial ruin. For now, he is satisfied about his principles, and he looks down on those who find the temptation too great to resist.

"Now tell me, Christopher. What is your definition of bribery?"

"Well, let's see....The use of improper influence."

"Good. I suppose—"

"Bu the point is, there was no influence at all. The girl was going to be interviewed, anyway. She came voluntarily to have a good time. I cannot see that bribery is involved at all."

"Of course, I know you're not really serious."

"I am dead serious."

"But I'm surprised you cannot see that the same argument can be used for taking money. If the applicant is getting the job anyway, then there is no harm in accepting money from him."

...

"You see, the difference is this." He paused. "Let's put it this way. No man wants to part with his money. If you accept money from a man you make him poorer. But if you go to bed with a girl who asks for it, I don't see that you have done any harm." (12.52-58; 61)

Thought: Christopher suggests something that Obi recognizes as fundamentally dishonest: if you already know that a girl is appearing before the Scholarship Board, then it is not using improper influence to sleep with her if she offers. But, of course, she doesn't know that she's already qualified to appear before the Scholarship Board. On the other hand, Christopher does feel that it is improper to take money because you're relieving a man from something he needs (or wants) to keep. Money and sex are fundamentally different for Christopher, but Obi sees the dishonesty in each action.

She didn't throw it away, but went outside to his car and dropped it in the glove box. She came back and, holding out her hand in mock facetiousness, said: "Thank you very much for everything."

"Come sit down, Clara. Let's not be childish. And please don't make things more difficult for me."

"You are making things difficult for yourself. How many times did I tell you that we were deceiving ourselves? But I as always told I was being childish. Anyway, it doesn't matter. There is no need for a long talk." (15.22-24)

Thought: When Clara realizes her relationship with Obi is over, she tries to explain to Obi that he lied to her throughout their relationship. She had always known that it couldn't work, that his family would never allow it. No only did he lie throughout their relationship that it would work, he is *still* lying to her even as she gives her ring back.

He rose to his feet, placed the wad of notes on the occasional table before Obi. "This is just small kola," he said. "We will make good friends. Don't forget the name. We will see again. Do you ever go to the club? I have never seen you before."

"I'm not a member."

"You must join," he said. "Bye-bye."

The wad of notes lay where he had placed it for the rest of the day and all night. Obi placed a newspaper over it and secured the door. "This is terrible!" he muttered. "Terrible!" he said aloud...

Obi steered her towards his bedroom. She made a halfhearted show of resisting, then followed.

Obviously she was not an innocent schoolgirl. She knew her job. She was on the short list already, anyway....

Others came. People would say that Mr. So-and-so was a gentleman. He would take money, but he would do his stuff, which was a big advertisement, and others would follow. But Obi stoutly refused to countenance anyone who did not possess the minimum educational and other requirements. On that he was unshakeable. (19.18-24)

Thought: After his mother's death and his broken engagement with Clara, Obi begins to accept bribes left and right. It is not so much that his principles have changed, but rather that he seems to have given up. He no longer thinks it's possible to remain pure, so wonders why he should even try. Yet despite all of that, he still retains some semblance of his principles, and refuses to accept bribes from those who don't have a chance in the first place. Ironically, it just brings more bribes to his doorstep, since he earns the reputation of following through with the bribes.

Society and Class Quotes

"The guests then said their farewells to Obi, many of them repeating all the advice that he had already been given. They shook hands with him and as they did so they pressed their presents into his palm, to buy a pencil with, or an exercise book or a loaf of bread for the journey, a shilling there and a penny there – substantial presents in a village where money was so rare, where men and women toiled from year to year to wrest a meager living from an unwilling and exhausted soil. (1.51)

Thought: The men and women of Umuofia may suffer from poverty, but they are generous with their gifts when Obi departs for England. These kinsmen are investing in Obi, hoping he will help lift their village out of poverty when he returns with a college education.

It was from one of these soldiers that Obi had his first picture of Lagos.

"There is no darkness there," he told his admiring listeners, "because at night the electric shines like the sun, and people are always walking about, that is, those who want to walk. If you don't want to walk you only have to wave your hand and a pleasure car stops for you." His audience made sounds of wonderment. Then by way of digression he said: "If you see a white man, take off your hat for him. The only thing he cannot do is mold a human being." (2.3-4)

Thought: The soldier paints a world of privilege, and highlights things that the rural citizens of Nigeria are lacking. We can see that urban citizens have greater privileges and access to more of the luxuries of modernization than rural citizens; but we also see that whites rule society.

They drove for awhile in silence through narrow overcrowded streets. "I can't understand why you should choose your dressmaker from the slums." Clara did not reply. Instead she started humming "Che sarà sarà."(2.19)

Thought: Early in his career in the civil service, Obi has assumed the values of upper-class society, while Clara still appreciates a bargain. (This will show up later, when it becomes clear that Obi has no clue how to manage his money, while Clara is adept at making her salary go a long way.) There is some irony in the song Clara hums – "Whatever will be will be" – His original name, which we know fromjuxtaposed with Obi's pretensions. Perhaps she already envisions that their relationship will end, since she is *osu* and Obi is already firmly entrenched in Igbo values.

"But take one of these old men. He probably left school thirty years ago in Standard Six. He has worked steadily to the top through bribery—an ordeal by bribery. To him the bribe is natural. He gave it and he expects it. Our people say that if you pay homage to the man on top, others will pay homage to you when it is your turn to be on top. Well, that is what the old men say." (2.31)

Thought: The corruption in Nigeria can partly be explained by the fact that Igbo society is built on a system of homage and patronage. These values seem to have been carried over into the Western system.

He spoke of the great honor Obi had brought to the ancient town of Umuofia, which could not join the comity of other towns in their march towards political irredentism, social equality, and economic emancipation.

"The importance of having one of our sons in the vanguard of this march of progress is nothing short of axiomatic." (4.15-16)

Thought: The town of Umuofia clearly pins its hopes for economic power and social status in the education of its young men; the example of Obi Okonkwo is a case in point. What is interesting is that it seems like a version of socialism helps individuals advance within the larger capitalist society; in order for everyone to rise in the social class, they must invest in individuals.

Why did Clara insist that he must not tell his people about her yet? Could it be that she had not quite made up her mind to marry him? That could hardly be. She was as anxious as himself to be formally engaged, only she said he should not go to the expense of buying a ring until he had got a job. Perhaps she wanted to tell her people first. But if so, why all the mystery? Why had she not simply said that she was going to consult her people? Or maybe she was not as guileless as he had assumed and was using this suspense to bind him more strongly to her. Obi examined each possibility in turn and rejected it. (5.46)

Thought: In his first realization that there is something Clara hasn't told him, Obi begins to get suspicious; he just can't believe that his beloved would be deceitful.

"As a man comes into this world," he [Ogbuefi Odogwu] often said, "so will he go out of it. When a titled man dies, his anklets of title are cut so that he will return as he came. The Christians are right when they say that as it was in the beginning it will be in the end." 5.89

Thought: Though hierarchical structures may be part of Igbo (and colonial society), there are no distinctions made among individuals when death comes calling.

"What the matter, Clara? Tell me." He was no longer unruffled. There was a hint of tears in his voice.

"I am an osu," she wept. Silence. She stopped weeping and quietly disengaged herself form him. Still he said nothing.

"So you see we cannot get married," she said, quite firmly, almost gaily—a terrible kind of gaiety. Only the tears showed she had wept.

"Nonsense!" said Obi. He shouted it almost, as if by shouting it now he could wipe away those seconds of silence, when everything had seemed to stop, waiting in vain for him to speak. (7.62-64)

Thought: Obi has fallen in love with a woman who can never be part of his social class – she belongs to the lowest possible class, an untouchable caste. And though he denies that it bothers him, a moment of silence betrays uncertainty on his part.

Obi felt very sorry for her [Elsie Mark]. She was obviously an intelligent girl who had set her mind, like so many other young Nigerians, on university education. And who could blame them? Certainly not Obi. It was rather sheer hypocrisy to ask if a scholarship was as important as all that or if a university education was worth it. Every Nigerian knew the answer. It was yes.

A university degree was the philosopher's stone. It transmuted a third-class clerk on one hundred and fifty a year into a senior civil servant on five hundred and seventy, with car and luxuriously furnished quarters at nominal rent. And the disparity in salary and amenities did not tell even half the story. To occupy a "European post" was second only to actually being a European. (9.72-73.)

Thought: Education is the key to belonging to the new social class. To be considered a European would be enormously attractive. For sixty plus years, Europeans had controlled business, politics, education, and religion in Nigeria; their status was built at the expense of the Igbo people.

Family Quotes

In recent weeks the [Umuofia Progressive] Union had met several times over Obi Okonkwo's case. At the first meeting, a handful of people had expressed the view that there was no reason why the Union should worry itself over the troubles of a prodigal son who had shown great disrespect to it only a little while ago…

This view, although accepted as largely true, was not taken very seriously. For, as the President pointed out, a kinsman in trouble had to be saved, not blamed; anger against a brother was felt in the flesh, not in the bone. And so the Union decided to pay for the services of a lawyer from their funds. (1.29; 31)

Thought: Despite the bad blood between Obi Okonkwo and his union of fellow expatriates from Umuofia, the men support him because he is family. These Africans, who are less educated than Obi, had a stronger sense of ethnic ties than Obi.

"The guests then said their farewells to Obi, many of them repeating all the advice that he had already been given. They shook hands with him and as they did so they pressed their presents into his palm, to buy a pencil with, or an exercise book or a loaf of bread for the journey, a shilling there and a penny there—substantial presents in a village where money was so rare,

where men and women toiled from year to year to wrest a meager living from an unwilling and exhausted soil. (1.51)

Thought: The men and women of Umuofia are generous with their gifts when Obi departs for England. Part of the reason for this generosity is that because they are investing in Obi, whom they see as their collective child.

"Yes," said Obi. "Many black men who got the white man's country marry their women."

"You hear?" asked Matthew. "I tell you I have seen it with my own two eyes in Onitsha. The woman even had two children. But what happened in the end? She left those children and went back to her country. That is why I say a black man who marries a white woman wastes his time. Her stay with him is like the stay of the moon in the sky. When the time comes, she will go."

"Very true," said another man who had also traveled. "It is not her going away that matters. It is her turning the man's face away from his kinsmen while she stays."

"I am happy that you returned home safe," said Matthew to Obi.

"He is a son of Iguedo," said old Odogwu. "There are nine villages in Umuofia, but Iguedo is Iguedo. We have our faults, but we are not empty men who become white when they see white, and black when they see black." (5.96-101)

Thought: Obi feels the pride of familial connection and kinship, not realizing that his own engagement to Clare will cause the same (or worse) consternation as marrying a white woman.

Obi felt better and more confident in his decision now that there was an opponent, the first of hundreds to come, no doubt. Perhaps it was not a decision really; for him there could be only one choice. It was scandalous that in the middle of the twentieth century a man could be barred from marrying a girl simply because her great-great-great-great-grandfather had been dedicated to serve a god, thereby setting himself apart and turning his descendents into a forbidden caste to the end of Time. Quite unbelievable. And here was an educated man telling Obi he did not understand. "Not even my mother can stop me," he said as he lay down beside Joseph. (7.73)

Thought: Obi finds his sudden defensive position exhilarating and decides to override any objections to marrying Clara, even if his mother disapproves. Unfortunately, he won't be able to sustain this decision.

Obi knew better than anyone else that his family would violently oppose the idea of marrying an osu. Who wouldn't? But for him it was either Clara or nobody. Family ties were all very well as long as they did not interfere with Clara. "If I could convince my mother," he thought, "all would be well." (7.108)

Thought: Obi plans to forsake his family for Clara. While there may be a biblical principle that he can quote to his Christian father down the line, it is not an Igbo custom at all. He hopes that he can get his mother on his side.

"Let joking pass," said the old man who had earlier on greeted Umuofia in a warlike salute. "Joshua is now without a job. We have given him ten pounds. But ten pounds does not talk. If you stand a hundred pounds here where I stand now, it will not talk. That is why we say that he who has people is richer than he who has money. Everyone of us here should look out for openings in his department and put in a word for Joshua. This was greeted with approval. (8.24)

Thought: Though Joshua needs money for a bribe in order to get a job, he also needs connections. The old man speaking here demonstrates one of the principles operating throughout Africa: kinship ties. Kinship ties dictate your obligations to people from your clan or village. In this case, kinship ties will allow Joshua to find a job. This principle, called *nepotism*, is one of the operating principles in modern Nigerian politics and business, as presented in this novel.

Clara begged him not to misunderstand her. She said she was taking her present step because she did not want to ruin his life. "I have thought about the whole matter very carefully. There are two reasons why we should not get married."

"What are they?"

"Well, the first is that your family will be against it. I don't want to come between you and your family."

"Bunk! Anyway, what is the second reason?" She could not remember what it was. It didn't matter, anyway. The first reason was quite enough. (13. 7-10)

Thought: In African cultures, the family is intimately involved in the selection of the spouse and in the continuation of the marriage.

He that has a brother must hold him to his heart,
For a kinsman cannot be bought in the market,
Neither is a brother bought with money. (13. 36)

Thought: Obi hears the lyrics of this song sung when he is waiting to hear what his ill mother has to say to him about his engagement to Clara, an *osu*. The song suggests two significant things: 1) that family is the most important thing; and 2) that no matter what you do for you're your family, you cannot make them obligated to you through material items. Though Obi has in the past suggested that if he can just convince his mother to accept Clara, it will be OK, this song suggests that can never be obligated to support his desire to marry a woman whom he is forbidden to marry.

"How were all our people in Lagos when you left them?" he asked. He sat on his wooden bed while Obi sat on a low stool facing him, drawing lines with his finger on the dusty top of the Harvest table.

"Lagos is a very big place. You can travel the distance from here to Abame and still be in Lagos."

"So they said. But you have a meeting of Umuofia people?" It was half-question, half-statement.

"Yes. We have a meeting. But it is only once a month." And he added: "It is not always that one finds time to attend." The fact was he had not attended since November.

"True," said his father. "But in a strange land one should always move near one's kinsmen." (14. 8-12)

Thought: Obi's father Isaac gently reminds him that not only is it a duty to associate with one's fellow citizens and relatives when one lives a long distance away from home, but it is a necessity. Family is what gives an individual their identity, their security, their community away from home.

Obi had done his best to make the whole thing sound unimportant. Just a temporary setback and no more. Everything would work out nicely in the end. His mothers' mind had been affected by her long illness but she would soon get over it. AS for his father, he was as good as won over. "All we need do is lie quiet for a little while," he said.

Clara had listened in silence, rubbing her engagement ring with her right fingers. When he stopped talking, she looked up at him and asked if he had finished.

...

"What are you talking about, Clara?...Oh, don't be silly," he said as she pulled off her ring and held it out to him.

"If you don't take it, I shall throw it out of the window." (15.12-13;19-20)

Thought: Though he would like to believe otherwise, Obi is not ready to forsake his family for the woman he loves. He tries to make it sound like he is not breaking up with Clara, but she knows the truth.

Marriage Quotes

"Today we send you [Obi] to bring knowledge. Remember that the fear of the Lord is the beginning of wisdom. I have heard of young men from other towns who went to the white man's country, but instead of facing their studies they went after the sweet things of the flesh. Some of them even married white women." The crowd murmured its strong disapproval of such behavior.

"A man who does that is lost to his people. He is like rain wasted in the forest. I should have suggested getting you a wife before you leave. Bu the time is too short now. Anyway, I know that we have no fear where you are concerned. We are sending you to learn book. Enjoyment can wait. Do not be in a hurry to rush into the pleasures of the world like the young antelope who danced herself lame when the main dance was yet to come." (1.48)

Thought: Before Obi leaves for England, his elders caution him against sex and wild ways, wishing that he was already married. They hope he won't come back with a white wife. Although there is no mention of *osus* in this passage, we are given a clear picture of certain marriages as taboo.

"When you have paid a hundred and thirty pounds bride-price and you are only a second-class clerk, you find you haven't got any more to spare on other women."

"You mean you paid a hundred and thirty? What about the bride-price law?"

"It pushed up the price, that's all."

"It's a pity my three elder sisters got married too early for us to make money on them. We'll try and make up on the others."

"It's no laughing matter," said Joseph. "Wait until you want to marry. They will probably ask you to pay five hundred, seeing that you are in the senior service."

"....I'm not paying five hundred pounds for a wife. I shall not even pay one hundred, not even fifty."

"You are not serious," said Joseph. "Unless you are going to be a Reverend Father." (5.25-31)

Thought: Joseph and Obi discuss marriage traditions in Nigeria. Marriage is seen as an exchange of money or goods from the groom's family to the bride's family. This tradition represents an agreement between families, and transfers the reproductive capacities of the woman to the husband's family so that children are considered part of his lineage rather than the lineage of the bride's family. Obi dismisses the tradition, indicating he has no intend to honor it, but Joseph lets him know that means he will never get married. He might as well be a priest.

Why did Clara insist that he must not tell his people about her yet? Could it be that she had not quite made up her mind to marry him? That could hardly be. She was as anxious as himself to be formally engaged, only she said he should not go to the expense of buying a ring until he had got a job. Perhaps she wanted to tell her people first. But if so, why all the mystery? Why had she not simply said that she was going to consult her people? Or maybe she was not as guileless as he had assumed and was using this suspense to bind him more strongly to her. Obi examined each possibility in turn and rejected it. (5.46)

Thought: Obi is anxious to tell his parents that he has found a woman to be his wife and the mother of his children. But Clara is hiding something, and it is only a matter of time before he finds out why she isn't eager for him to tell his parents about her. This is our first inclination that not all is well. Although Obi is aware something is wrong, he can't believe anything too negative about his beloved.

"Yes," said Obi. "Many black men who go t the white man's country marry their women."

"You hear?" asked Matthew. "I tell you I have seen it with my own two eyes in Onitsha. The woman even had two children. But what happened in the end? She left those children and went back to her country. That is why I say a black man who marries a white woman wastes his time. Her stay with him is like the stay of the moon in the sky. When the time comes, she will go."

"Very true," said another man who had also traveled. "It is not her going away that matters. It is her turning the man's face away from his kinsmen while she stays." (5.96-98)

Thought: The men of Umuofia indicate that the problem with a son of Umuofia marrying a woman from another culture is that she divides the son from his family. Marriage, in Igbo culture, is something that the families must agree upon. Furthermore, marriage should not divide a son from his parents.

"I can't marry you," she said suddenly...

"I don't understand you, Clara." And he really didn't. Was this woman's game to bind him more firmly? But Clara was not like that; she had no coyness in her....

"Why can't you marry me?" He succeeded in sounding unruffled. For answer she threw herself at him and began to weep violently on his shoulder.

"What the matter, Clara? Tell me." He was no longer unruffled. There was a hint of tears in his voice.

"I am an osu," she wept. Silence. She stopped weeping and quietly disengaged herself form him. Still he said nothing.

"So you see we cannot get married," she said, quite firmly, almost gaily—a terrible kind of gaiety. Only the tears showed she had wept.

"Nonsense!" said Obi. He shouted it almost, as if by shouting it now he could wipe away those seconds of silence, when everything had seemed to stop, waiting in vain for him to speak. (7.58-64)

Thought: In the first of many scenes where Clara tells Obi she cannot marry him, she admits her status as part of a forbidden caste. And though Obi is quick to say that it doesn't matter, the few seconds of silence indicate that it *does* matter. He may want to throw off some of the more inconvenient parts of his culture, but he knows that his friends and family will not be so accommodating.

"I am going to marry her," Obi said.

"What?" Joseph sat up in bed.

"I am going to marry her."

"Look at me," said Joseph..."You know book, but this is no matter for book. Do you know what an osu is? But how can you know?" In that short question he said in effect that Obi's mission-house upbringing and European education had made him a stranger in his country—the most painful thing one could say to Obi.

I know more about it than yourself," he said, "and I'm going to marry the girl. I wasn't actually seeking your approval." (7.67-71)

Thought: Obi decides to go completely against his culture's norms, traditions, and values by marrying Clara. Obi bristles when Joseph claims he must be ignorant of those customs and values. And he's not ignorant of those values, but the tradition of an untouchable caste is something he feels should be destroyed. Should his identity as an African be called into question simply because he recognizes that a certain cultural value is wrong?

They went in the car and made for the jeweler's shop in Kingsway and bought a twenty-pound ring....

"What about a Bible?" Clara asked.

"What Bible?"

"To go with the ring. Don't you know that?"

Obi didn't know that. They went over to the C.M.S. Bookshop and paid for a handsome little Bible with a zip. (7.80-84)

Thought: Though Obi and Clara are now engaged in the European way, it is not an engagement that is recognized in Igbo culture. A marriage isn't recognized in Igbo culture until the bride-price is arranged. The bride-price is an arrangement of goodwill that links the two families, and transfers the bride's reproductive capacities from her father's lineage to the husband's lineage.

"By the way, we are now engaged. I gave her a ring this afternoon."

"Very good," said Joseph bitterly. He thought for a while and then asked: "Are you going to marry the English way or are you going to ask your people to approach her people according to custom?"

"I don't know yet. It depends on what my father says."

"Did you tell him about it during your visit?"

"No, because I hadn't decided then."

"He will not agree to it," said Joseph. "Tell anyone that I said so."

"I can handle them," said Obi, "especially my mother."

"Look at me, Obi." Joseph invariably asked people to look at him. "What you are going to do concerns not only yourself but your whole family and future generations. If one finger brings oil it soils the others. In future, when we are all civilized, anybody may marry anybody. But that time has not come. We of this generation are only pioneers." (7.97-104)

Thought: Joseph insists that marrying an *osu* is like staining a shirt with oil. It is not just the little bit of cloth that is ruined; the entire shirt is tainted. Though Obi would like to change the customs, the time has not arrived for that. If he persists and marries Clara, it will only bring grief to himself, his family, and his children.

"We are Christians," he [Isaac] said. "But that is no reason to marry an osu."

"The Bible says that in Christ there are no bond or free."

"My son," said Okonkwo, "I understand what you say. But this thing is deeper than you think."

...

"Osu is like leprosy in the minds of our people. I beg of you, my son, not to bring the mark of shame and of leprosy into your family. If you do, your children and your children's children unto the third and fourth generations will curse your memory. It is not for myself I speak; my days are few. You will bring sorrow on your head and on the heads of your children. Who will marry your daughters? Whose daughters will your sons marry? Think of that, my son. We are Christians, but we cannot marry our own daughters." (14. 33-35;38)

Thought: Though Isaac Okonkwo understands Obi's arguments that there should not be a class of citizens marked as untouchables, he says that their family must live within the larger society. And within the larger society, there is this class of untouchables. Religious, philosophical, and logical arguments have their place, but they cannot change larger society.

She stopped and took a deep breath. "I have nothing to tell you in this matter except one thing. If you want to marry this girl, you must wait until I am no more. If God hears my prayers, you will not wait long." She stopped again. Obi was terrified by the change that had come over her. She looked strange as if she had suddenly gone off her head.

"Mother!" he called, as if she was going away. She held up her hand for silence.

"But if you do the thing while I am alive, you will have my blood on your head, because I shall kill myself." She sank down completely exhausted. (14. 47-49)

Thought: To marry an *osu* is one of the worst taboos in Igbo culture. Obi's hope that he might be able to get his mother on his side is dashed forever when she threatens suicide if he marries her before she dies. Obi may have believed that, as Christians, his parents would be more flexible, but he failed to take into account how deeply immersed they are in their own culture.

Dreams, Hopes, Plans Quotes

Six or seven years ago Umuofians abroad had formed their Union with the aim of collecting money to send some of their brighter young men to study in England. They taxed themselves mercilessly. (1.39)

Thought: The hopes and dreams of Umuofians rest on the education of their sons, collectively. Education is the best way to bring honor and money to their home village.

Almost immediately, a cyclist crossed the road without looking back or giving any signal. Obi jammed on his brakes and his tires screamed on the tarmac. Clara let out a little scream and gripped his left arm. The cyclist looked back once and rode away, his ambition written for all to see on his black bicycle bag—FUTURE MINISTER. (2.21)

Thought: As they leave the slums, Obi almost hits a man on a bicycle. The cyclist's desire for an ambitious future represents a major theme of *No Longer At Ease*. According to the novel, we learn that, in Nigeria, anybody can become something if he is able and willing to play the game of bribery and corruption.

"Iguedo breeds great men," said Odogwu, changing the subject…." Today greatness has changed its tune. Titles are no longer great, neither are barns or large numbers o wives and children. Greatness is now in the things of the white man. And so we too have changed our tune. We are the first in all the nine villages to send our son to the white man's land. Greatness has belonged to Iguedo from ancient times. It is not made by man. You cannot plant greatness as you plant yams or maize. Who ever planted an iroko tree –the greatest tree in the forest? You may collect all the iroko seeds in the world, open the soil and put them there. It will be in vain. The great tree chooses where to grow and we find it there, so it is with greatness in men." (5.108)

Thought: The men of Umuofia see their destiny in this young man, Obi Okonkwo, who represents the fulfillment of their dreams. Part of Obi's fulfillment of that dream will be to embrace Western culture. In one sense, fulfilling these dreams necessarily means being alienated from his own people, though they do not yet see that.

"Last year," she said suddenly, "none of the girls in our school who got Grade One was given a scholarship."

"Perhaps they did not impress the Board."

"It wasn't that. It was because they did not see the members at home."

"So you intend to see the members?"

"Yes."

"Is a scholarship as important as all that? Why doesn't a relation of yours pay for you to go to a university?"

....

Obi felt very sorry for her [Elsie Mark]. She was obviously an intelligent girl who had set her mind, like so many other young Nigerians, on university education. And who could blame them? Certainly not Obi. It was rather sheer hypocrisy to ask if a scholarship was as important as all that or if a university education was worth it. Every Nigerian knew the answer. It was yes. (9.63-68;72.)

Thought: Elsie's hopes and dreams rest in getting a university education, and she's willing to give up a lot of herself in order to get it. Why does she go to such extremes? Because if she does, she will never be dependent on a man every again – she and her family – but instead, she will be in the position of bestowing favors.

[Mr Green] turned to Obi and said: "you know, Okonkwo, I have lived in your country for fifteen years and yet I cannot begin to understand the mentality of the so-called educated Nigerian. Like this young man at the University College, for instance, who expects the Government not only to pay his fees and fantastic allowances and find him an easy, comfortable job at the end of his course, but also to pay his intended. It's absolutely incredible. I think Government is making a terrible mistake in making it so easy for people like that to have so-called University education. Education for what? To get as much as they can for themselves and their family. Not the last bit interested in the millions of their countrymen who die every day from hunger and disease." (12.6)

Thought: Though education is a way for Nigerians to achieve their hopes and dreams, Mr. Green suggests it is also an easy way for them to milk the system. Read Mr. Green's "Character Analysis" for more on his beliefs and the role he plays in *No Longer At Ease*.

[Obi] told [Christopher] of one old catechist in Umuofia many, many years ago when Obi was a little boy. This man's wife was a very good friend of Obi's mother and often visited them. One day he overheard her telling his mother how her education had been cut short at Standard One because the man was impatient to get married. She sounded very bitter about it, although it must have happened at least twenty years before. Obi remembered this particular visit very well because it took place on a Saturday. On the following morning the catechist had been unable to take the service because his wife had broken his head with the wooden pestle used for pounding yams. (12.34)

Thought: It doesn't seem like Obi is deliberately advocating a feminist ideology here, rather he is suggesting that an unhappy wife is dangerous. It is better to let her do what she wants to do than get in the way.

The book opened at the place where he had put the paper on which he had written the poem "Nigeria" in London about two years ago.

God bless our noble fatherland
Great land of sunshine bright,
Where brave men chose the way of peace,
To win their freedom fight.
May we preserve our purity,
Our zest for life and jollity.
God bless our noble countrymen
And women everywhere.
Teach them to walk in unity
To build our nation dear;
Forgetting region, tribe or speech,
But caring always each for each.
London, July 1955.

He quietly and calmly crumpled the paper in his left palm until it was a tiny ball, threw it on the floor, and began to turn the pages of the book forwards and backwards. In the end he did not read any poem. He put the book down on the little table by his bed. (16.28-30)

Thought: This poem makes reference the bright shiny dreams Obi once had for his country, dreams that now seem tarnished due to his own personal failings in life, finances, family, and love.

When Obi came out, one of the patients was waiting to have a word with him.

"You tink because Government give you car you fit do what you like? You see all of we de wait here and you just go in. You tink na play we come play?"

Obi passed on without saying a word.

"Foolish man. He tink say because him get car so derefore he can do as he like. Beast of no nation." (16.36-39)

Thought: One man who resents the wealth and privilege that Obi enjoys suggests that wealth and privilege also bring selfishness and disrespect. Obi has become like the men he used to despise.

As he turned these things over in his mind the door opened and a messenger entered. Involuntarily Obi jumped to his feet to accept an envelope. He looked it over and turned it round and saw that it had not been opened. He put it in his shirt pocket and sank to his seat....

His decision to write to Clara had been taken last night....

Obi, who nowadays spent all his time in bed, had got himself out and gone to his writing desk. Writing letters did not come easily to him. He worked out every sentence in his mind first before he set it down on paper. Sometimes he spent as long as ten minutes on the opening sentence. He wanted to say: "Forgive me for what has happened. It was all my fault..." He ruled again it; that kind of self-reproach was sheer humbug. In the end he wrote:

"I can understand your not wanting ever to set eyes on me again. I have wronged you terribly. But I cannot believe that it is all over. If you give me another chance, I shall never fail you again."

He read it over and over again. Then he rewrote the whole letter, changing I cannot believe to I cannot bring myself to believe. (17.31-35)

Thought: When Clara returns Obi's letter unopened, he has to force himself to realize that his dreams for their future together are over.

Love Quotes

They heard Macmillan bang his cabin door. Their eyes met for a second, and without another word Obi took her in his arms. She was trembling as he kissed her over and over again.

"Leave me," she whispered.

"I love you."

She was silent for a while, seeming to melt in his arms.

"You don't," she said suddenly. "We're only being silly. You'll forget it in the morning." She looked at him and then kissed him violently. "I know I'll hate myself in the morning." (3.64-68)

Thought: Though he barely knows Clara – and certainly doesn't know that she is part of a forbidden caste, the *osu* – Obi declares his love for her. Clara protests, in part because she knows things he doesn't.

Until Obi met Clara on board the cargo boat Sasa he had though of love as another grossly overrated European invention…There was always a part of him, the thinking part, which seemed to stand outside it all watching the passionate embrace with cynical disdain. The result was that one half of Obi might kiss a girl and murmur: "I love you," but the other half would say: "Don't be silly." And it was always this second half that triumphed in the end when the glamour had evaporated with the heat, leaving a ridiculous anticlimax

With Clara it was different. It had been from the very first. There was never a superior half at Obi's elbow wearing a patronizing smile. (7.56-57)

Thought: Without knowing much about Clara or her family, Obi has thrown himself head first into a passionate love affair. This kind of love affair is similar to romance in Western culture and indicates that Obi and Clara may have adopted some Western values.

He knew that many of these secretaries were planted to spy on Africans. One of their tactics was to pretend to be very friendly and broad-minded. One had to watch what one said….

As the weeks passed, however, Obi's guard began to come down "small small," as they say. It started with Clara's visit to his office one morning to tell him something or other. Miss Tomlinson had heard her voice on the telephone a few times and had commented on its attractiveness. Obi introduced them, and was a little surprised at the English woman's genuine delight. When Clara left she talked about nothing else for the rest of the day. "Isn't she beautiful? Aren't you lucky? When are you getting married? I shouldn't wait if I were you," and so on and so forth.

Obi felt like a clumsy schoolboy earning his first praise for doing something extraordinarily clever. He began to see Miss Tomlinson in a different light. If it was part of her tactics, it was really a very clever one for which she deserved credit. But it did not look clever or forced. It seemed to have come straight from her heart. (9.3-5)

Thought: Obi's love for Clara makes him receptive to Mr. Green's secretary, who is likely spying on Obi to see if he does anything wrong. Miss Tomlinson is able to practice her deceit (and might be involved in Obi's later downfall) because she flatters him about Clara.

For some reason he knew, despite the size of the parcel, that it contained his ring. And some money too! Yes, five-pound notes. But he didn't see any ring. He signed with relief and then read the little note enclosed.

Darling, I'm sorry about yesterday. Go to the bank straight away and cancel that overdraft. See you in the evening. Love, Clara.

His eyes misted. (11.14-16)

Thought: Obi thought he was alone in solving his bad financial situation. He thought Clara would break up with him over his irresponsible financial planning. But it turns out Clara wants to be his partner in financial matters as well. This situation also reveals how little Obi knows about love and partnership.

That evening they called on Christopher, Obi's economist friend. Clara had gradually come round to liking him. Perhaps he was a little too lively, which was not a serious fault. But she feared he might influence Obi for the worse in the matter of women. He seemed to enjoy going around with four or five at once. He even said there was nothing like love, at any rate in Nigeria. (11.34)

Thought: Christopher's willingness to go around with more than one woman might reflect the way the traditional culture of polygamy meets the modern European custom of dating.

Nylon dress is a lovely dress,
nylon dress is a country dress.
If you want to make your baby happy
Nylon is good for her.
...
If you want to make your baby happy
Go to the shop and get a doz'n of nylon.
She will know nobody but you alone
Nylon is good for you.
(11.66;70)

Thought: The theme of this song suggests that love is shown through material items. In Western ideology, love is idealized in such a way that material concerns are rarely considered a part of it. But traditionally, in western Africa, love is shown through giving gifts that enable a woman to live. Since women are the ones primarily responsible for feeding their families through subsistence farming, a husband in this culture doesn't have the same responsibilities that a husband in Europe or the United States has. Instead, men here give women aesthetically pleasing gifts that they couldn't get through their own farming and trading efforts.

Obi had been shocked by the crudity of Christopher's reaction to his story. ...

"You know, Obi," he said, "I had wanted to discuss that matter with you. But I have learnt not to interfere in a matter between a man and a woman, especially with chaps like you who have wonderful ideas about love...That was why I didn't tell you anything about Clara. You may say that I am not broad-minded, but I don't think we have reached the stage where we can ignore all our customs. You may talk about education and so on, but I am not going to marry an osu." (15.32-33)

Thought: Christopher argues with Obi that love is not enough to overcome stigma and familial opposition. Essentially, he's saying that Romeo and Juliet is a wonderful story, but in real life, love needs more than romance to sustain it. Furthermore, he suggests, even though colonialism, Christianity, and Western education have changed Igbo culture, there are some cultural traditions that remain no matter what. These cultural traditions – such as not marrying an *osu* – will always trump love.

"Why don't you marry the girl anyway? She is very good-looking."

"I don't want to marry him," said Clara sullenly, the first thing she had said since they came in

"What's wrong with him? He seems a nice young man to me."

"I say I won't marry him. Isn't that enough?" she almost screamed, and rushed out of the room. Obi went quietly after her and they drove off. No single word passed between them all the way to the house of the next doctor who had been recommended to Obi. (15.49-52)

Thought: When Obi seeks an abortion for Clara, he discovers that Clara's mind is already made up –whatever love they had for each other is gone, and with it, their commitment to marry.

As he sat in the driver's seat, paralyzed by his thoughts, the doctor and Clara came out and entered a car that was parked by the side of the road. The doctor must have said something about him because Clara looked in his direction once and immediately took her eyes away. Obi wanted to rush out of his car and shout: "Stop. Let's go and get married now," but he couldn't' and didn't. The doctor's car drove away. (16.17)

Thought: In the end, Obi's love for Clara is not strong enough to overcome their difficult situation.

"Don't worry, she will be all right. But I want to have her under observation tonight in case of complications."

"Can't I see her?"

"No. Tomorrow morning. That is, if she wants to see you. Women are very funny creatures, you

know." (16.20-22)

Thought: Neither the doctor nor Obi can understand how an abortion has the potential to change the way a woman looks on the man she once loved.

Principles Quotes

The oldest man present [of the Umuofia Progressive Union] broke one of them [kola nuts], saying another kind of prayer while he did it. "He that brings kola nuts brings life," he said. "We do not seek to hurt any man, but if any man seeks to hurt us may he break his neck." The congregation answered Amen. "We are strangers in this land. If good comes to it may we have our share." Amen. "But if bad comes let it go to the owners of the land who know what gods should be appeased." (1.37)

Thought: The men of Umuofia Progressive Union express their guiding principles here: that all good things come to them, and that bad things fall on others.

"The civil service is corrupt because of these so-called experienced men at the top," said Obi.

"You don't believe in experience? You think that a chap straight from university should be made a permanent secretary?"

"I didn't say straight from the university, but even that would be better than filling our top posts with old men who have no intellectual foundations to support their experience."...

"To most of them [educated young men] bribery is no problem. They come straight to the top without bribing anyone. It's not that they're necessarily better than others, it's simply that they can afford to be virtuous. But even that kind of virtue can become a habit." (2.27-29; 33)

Thought: Obi expresses his opinion that education breeds principles, in part because it offers opportunities that people would otherwise lack. If you lack those educational opportunities, but you still have ambition, you must seek advancement through corrupt methods.

Customs formalities here took thrice as long as at Liverpool and five times as many officials. A young man, almost a boy in fact, was dealing with Obi's cabin. He told him that the duty on his radiogram would be five pounds.

"Right," said Obi, feeling his hip pockets. "Write a receipt for me." The boy did not write. He looked at Obi for a few seconds, and then said: "I can be able to reduce it to two pounds for you."

"How?" asked Obi.

"I fit do it, but you no go get Government receipt."

For a few seconds Obi was speechless. Then he merely said: "Don't be silly. If there was a policeman here I would hand you over to him." (4.3-7)

Thought: Obi's return to Nigeria is immediately marked by corruption. He is approached by one of the customs officials for a bribe – but Obi clearly refrains, even though it will cost him more money.

"What department he de work?"

"Secretary to the Scholarship Board."

"'E go make plenty money there. Every student who wan' go England go de see am for house."

"'E no be like dat," said Joseph. "Him na gentleman. No fit take bribe."

"Na so," said the other in unbelief. (8.5-9)

Thought: Bribery and corruption are so integral to the operations of Nigerian government that Joseph's co-workers find it incredible that a young man like Obi doesn't take bribes.

"Let joking pass," said the old man who had earlier on greeted Umuofia in a warlike salute. "Joshua is now without a job. We have given him ten pounds. But ten pounds does not talk. If you stand a hundred pounds here where I stand now, it will not talk. That is why we say that he who has people is richer than he who has money. Everyone of us here should look out for openings in his department and put in a word for Joshua. This was greeted with approval. (8.24)

Thought: Though Joshua needs money for a bribe in order to get a job, he also needs connections. The old man speaking here demonstrates one of the principles operating throughout Africa: kinship ties. Kinship ties dictate your obligations to people from your clan or village. In this case, kinship ties will allow Joshua to find a job. Though in the west, we might not regard kinship ties in a positive light, it is one of the operating principles in modern Nigerian politics and business.

"Let joking pass," said the old man who had earlier on greeted Umuofia in a warlike salute. "Joshua is now without a job. We have given him ten pounds. But ten pounds does not talk. If you stand a hundred pounds here where I stand now, it will not talk. That is why we say that he who has people is richer than he who has money. Everyone of us here should look out for openings in his department and put in a word for Joshua. This was greeted with approval.

"Thanks to the Man Above," he continued, "we now have one of our sons in the senior service. We are not going to ask him to bring his salary to share among us. It is in little things like this that he can help us. It is our fault if we do not approach him…."

"Your words are very good," said the President. "We have the same thought in our minds. But we must give the young man time to look round first and know what is what."

The meeting supported the President by their murmurs. "Give the young man time." "Let him settle down." Obi felt very uneasy. But he knew they meant well. Perhaps it would not be too difficult to manage them. (8.24-27)

Thought: Obi wonders if the Igbo operating principle of helping kin will interfere with his own principles against nepotism and taking bribes, values that he absorbed through his Western education.

And he told her of Mr. Mark's visit to his office and gave her a detailed account of all that transpired between Miss Mark and himself before her arrival.

When he finished, Clara said nothing for a little while.

"Are you satisfied?" asked Obi.

"I think you were too severe on the man," she said.

"You think I should have encouraged him to talk about bribing me?"

"After all, offering money is not as bad as offering one's body. And yet you gave her a drink and a lift back to town." She laughed. "Na so this world be."

Obi wondered. (9.104-110)

Thought: Although Clara believes that prostitution is worse than bribery, Obi sees bribery as corruption and prostitution as a form of victimization. Hence, he finds Elsie's offer of prostitution sad, and believes that if he had acquiesced, he would have participated in her victimization. He sees bribery as a corrupt deal between two equally responsible partners.

[Mr Green] turned to Obi and said: "you know, Okonkwo, I have lived in your country for fifteen years and yet I cannot begin to understand the mentality of the so-called educated Nigerian. Like this young man at the University College, for instance, who expects the Government not only to pay his fees and fantastic allowances and find him an easy, comfortable job at the end of his course, but also to pay his intended. It's absolutely incredible. I think Government is making a terrible mistake in making it so easy for people like that to have so-called University education. Education for what? To get as much as they can for themselves and their family. Not the last bit interested in the millions of their countrymen who die every day from hunger and disease." (12.6)

Thought: According to Mr. Green, the educated Nigerian has no principles. Or rather, there is just one principle: get as much wealth as possible. This principle seems to be upheld regardless of the cost to impoverished Nigerians who must pay for their corrupt leaders and businessmen.

"You are the biggest ass in Nigeria," said Christopher, and they began a long argument on the nature of bribery.

"If a girl offers to sleep with you, that is not bribery," said Christopher.

"Don't be silly," replied Obi. "You mean you honestly cannot see anything wrong in taking advantage of a young girl straight from school who wants to go to a university?"

"You are being sentimental. A girl who comes the way she did is not an innocent little girl. It's like the story of a girl who was given a form to fill in. She put down her name and her age. But when she came to sex she wrote: 'Twice a week.'" (12.40-43)

Thought: Though Obi believes he would be victimizing a young girl by sleeping with her after she asked for his help in getting a scholarship, Christopher sees the young girl as taking charge of her own destiny.

"Did you have a good leave?" Mr. Green asked when he saw Obi....

"It often amazes me how you people can have the effrontery to ask for local leave. The idea of local leave was to give Europeans a break to go to a cool place like Jos or Buea. But today it is completely obsolete. But for an African like you, who has too many privileges as it is, to ask for two weeks to go on a swan, it makes me want to cry."

"It is not the fault of Nigerians," said Obi. "You devised these soft conditions for yourselves when every European was automatically in the senior service and every African automatically in the junior service. Now that a few of us have been admitted into the senior service, you turn round and blame us." (17.1-2; 9)

Thought: Obi states that it is hypocritical for a European to criticize Africans for taking advantage of the special privileges; Europeans created those same privileges for their own enjoyment when they were in power.

Isolation Quotes

Obi was away in England for a little under four years. He sometimes found it difficult to believe that it was as short as that. It seemed more like a decade than four years, what with the miseries of winter when his longing to return home took on the sharpness of physical pain. It was in England that Nigeria first became more than just a name to him. That was the first great thing that England did for him.

But the Nigeria he returned to was in many ways different form the picture he had carried in his mind during those four years. (2.1-2)

Thought: There is a lot of irony in Obi's homesickness. Alone in England during his education, Obi longs for his family, his culture, and his country. His has a romanticized picture of Nigeria, one formed during his period of isolation and his loneliness. Ironically, while he is being educated abroad, Obi is learning values that will eventually bring him to criticize his own culture. Be sure to check out Obi's "Character Analysis" for more on this.

Four years in England had filled Obi with a longing to be back in Umuofia. The feeling was sometimes so strong that he found himself feeling ashamed of studying English for his degree. He spoke Igbo whenever he had the least opportunity of doing so. Nothing gave him greater pleasure than to find another Igbo-speaking student in a London bus. But when he had to speak in English with a Nigerian student from another tribe he lowered his voice. It was humiliating to have to speak to one's countryman in a foreign language, especially in the presence of the proud owners of that language. They would naturally assume that one had no language of one's own. He wished they were here today to see. Let them come to Umuofia now and listen to the talk of men who made a great art of conversation. Let them come and see men and women and children who knew how to live, whose joy of life had not yet been killed by those who claimed to teach other nations how to live. (5.73)

Thought: Isolated in England, Obi felt shame when he met his fellow Nigerians and couldn't converse in an African language. It made him feel bereft of his culture and language. When he had an opportunity to speak Igbo with another African, he took it. Speaking Igbo made him feel less homesick, and allowed him to take pride in his African heritage.

Obi felt better and more confident in his decision now that there was an opponent, the first of hundreds to come, no doubt. Perhaps it was not a decision really; for him there could be only one choice. It was scandalous that in the middle of the twentieth century a man could be barred from marrying a girl simply because her great-great-great-great-grandfather had been dedicated to serve a god, thereby setting himself apart and turning his descendents into a forbidden caste to the end of Time. Quite unbelievable. And here was an educated man telling Obi he did not understand. "Not even my mother can stop me," he said as he lay down beside Joseph. (7.73)

Thought: Clara's family is isolated because of their social status. Because Obi willingly embraces Clara, he enters into his own kind of isolation. But the isolation caused by Joseph's disapproval – and the disapproval that will soon come from others, including his family – fills him with a sense of righteousness that gives him power and resolve.

And if one thought objectively of the matter...could one blame those poor men for being critical of a senior service man who appeared reluctant to pay twenty pounds a month? They had taxed themselves mercilessly to raise eighth hundred pounds to send him to England. Some of them earned no more than five pounds a month. He earned nearly fifty. They had wives and school going children; he had none. After paying the twenty pounds he would have thirty left. And very soon he would have an increment which alone was as big as some people's salary.

Obi admitted that his people had a sizable point. What they did not know was that, having labored in sweat and tears to enroll their kinsman among the shining elite, they had to keep him there. Having made him a member of an exclusive club whose members greet one another with "how's the car behaving?" did they expect him to turn round and answer: "I'm sorry, but my car is off the road. You see I couldn't pay my insurance premium"? That would be letting the side down in a way that was quite unthinkable. (10.16-17)

Thought: As the first member of his village to achieve status and money through a position in the senior service, Obi is on his own when it comes to dealing with the multitude of financial problems that come his way. His obligations to his family and the Progressive Union make it increasingly difficult for him to maintain his status. Furthermore, nobody in the Union can understand or see his point because nobody has ever been there before.

"Why didn't you tell me?" she asked when he had told her about the overdraft.

"Well, there was no need. I'll pay it easily in five monthly installments."

"That's not the point. You don't think I should be told when you're in difficulty."

"I wasn't in difficulty. I wouldn't have mentioned it if you hadn't pressed me." (10.39-42)

Thought: Obi is so used to dealing with his problems alone, that he doesn't even understand why Clara might be hurt that he hasn't confided in her.

"We are Christians," he [Isaac] said. "But that is no reason to marry an osu."

"The Bible says that in Christ there are no bond or free."

"My son," said Okonkwo, "I understand what you say. But this thing is deeper than you think."

[…]

"Osu is like leprosy in the minds of our people. I beg of you, my son, not to bring the mark of shame and of leprosy into your family. If you do, your children and your children's children unto the third and fourth generations will curse your memory. It is not for myself I speak; my days are few. You will bring sorrow on your head and on the heads of your children. Who will marry your daughters? Whose daughters will your sons marry? Think of that, my son. We are Christians, but we cannot marry our own daughters." (14. 33-35, 38)

Thought: If Obi marries Clara, his family will be alone in the world, isolated from the larger society. His children will not be able to marry. Though he can try to break the rules of society, society is less flexible than he thinks. And he cares more about his family's situation than he originally admits.

The chief result of the crisis in Obi's life was that it made him examine critically for the first time the mainspring of his actions. And in doing so he uncovered a good deal that he could only regard as sheer humbug. Take this matter of twenty pounds each month to his town union, which in the final analysis was the root cause of all his troubles. Why had he not swallowed his pride and accepted the four months' exemption which he had been allowed, albeit with a bad grace? Could a person in his position afford that kind of pride? Was it not a common saying among his people that a man should not, out of pride and etiquette, swallow his phlegm? (17.29)

Thought: Obi's pride has led him to take on too much responsibility. He is unwilling to accept others' help, no matter if the help is graciously or ungraciously offered. This has left him isolated and alone when he faces true crisis.

Everybody was most kind. Mr. Green said he could take a week's leave if he wished. Obi took two days He went straight home and locked himself up in his flat. What was the point in going to Umuofia? She would have been buried by the time he got there, anyway. The thought of going home and not finding her! In the privacy of his bedroom he let tears run down his face like a child. (18.21)

Thought: Although Obi could go home and share his family's sorrow, he chooses to remain in Lagos. His mother has been a moral compass in his life, his one link to traditional culture, and now he is desolate without her.

Before very long a number of Umuofia people began to arrive. Some came in taxis, not singly like Joseph but in teams of three or four, sharing the fare among them. Others came on bicycles. Altogether there were over twenty-five.

The president of the Umuofia Progressive Union asked whether it was permissible to sing hymns in Ikoyi. He asked because Ikoyi was a European reservation. Obi said he would rather they did not sing, but he was touched most deeply that so many of his people had come, in spite of everything, to condole with him. (18.30-331)

Thought: Obi is not so alone in his grief, after all. Despite his shabby treatment of his friends in Lagos, they join him in his sorrow over his mother's death.

Plot Analysis

Classic Plot Analysis

Initial Situation

The courtroom, the tennis club, meeting of the Umuofia Progressive Union

No Longer At Ease opens with Obi Okonkwo's corruption trial. Obi is presumed to be guilty by all sides, though the narrator doesn't seem to pass judgment. There are three important moments in the initial situation.

The first is when Obi is faced with the judge's comment that he can't understand how a man of such "education" and "brilliant promise" could have done with Obi did. Until that moment, Obi had tried to keep a stiff upper lip, but faced with this assessment of his character, he starts to cry.

The second pivotal moment is when Mr. Green, Obi's former boss, discusses the court case with a British friend. Mr. Green explains that all Africans are corrupt. He doesn't try to explain why or how they become corrupt, only that they are, and for this, he implies that they should never achieve self-governance.

The third moment is when the Umuofia Progressive Union meets and discusses Obi's case. They analyze the situation, saying it's "shameful" for Obi to go to prison when such a small amount of money is concerned (only twenty pounds), but admit that Obi's problem was that he accepted bribes without covering his tracks. According to the union, Obi foolishly assumed he was smarter than those who might try to uncover his corruption.

Conflict

Obi learns that Clara is osu and proposes to her despite knowledge that all of his kinsmen and his family will oppose the marriage.

Obi is surprised when Clara doesn't want him to tell his family about her, but soon he learns the truth: she is *osu*, and this fact – that she and her ancestors are dedicated to a god – prevents them from getting married, according to traditional custom. But Obi has been educated in England, and he works for a British governmental system, with many European colleagues. He's not about to let his traditional culture prevent him from marrying the woman he loves. Despite warnings from his friend Joseph, Obi and Clara become engaged.

Complication

Clara's money is stolen.

Obi soon discovers that he isn't a very good financial planner. When his car insurance becomes due, he has no money to pay it, so he takes a bank loan. Clara gives him fifty pounds so he can pay back the bank loan, but then her money is stolen while they go dancing in a nightclub. Obi begins to feel like things are slipping out of his control.

Climax

Obi's mother tells him that she will commit suicide if he marries Clara before she dies.
Obi receives a letter from his father, saying they would like him to visit as they have some important things to discuss. Obi realizes now that somebody has told them about Clara. Now he needs to come clean. He is certain he can convince his parents to support his marriage to Clara, since they are Christians and never followed Igbo religious customs. But his father, Isaac Okonkwo, simply tells him that he can't marry Clara; this marriage will bring shame on his head and on his children's heads. Obi's mother, Hannah Okonkwo, tells Obi that if he marries Clara while she is alive, she will commit suicide.

Suspense
Clara gets an abortion.
Obi tells Clara that his father is almost convinced to let them marry, but his mother needs more time. Clara realizes that he's lying, that their relationship is over. This is when Obi realizes that Clara is pregnant. He arranges for an abortion, going deeper into debt. When the two abortion doctors they visit ask him why he doesn't marry Clara, Clara snarls that she has no interest in marrying Obi. Clara's abortion turns septic, and she spends weeks in a hospital recovering. Obi tries to reignite their relationship by apologizing in writing, but Clara returns his letters unopened. When she is released from the hospital, she leaves Lagos.

Denouement
Obi's mother dies.
To top it off, Obi's mother dies. Now Obi has lost both the women he loves. He grieves his mother's death alone in his Lagos flat. He sends money home to pay for the funeral, but he does not return home to be with his family.

Conclusion
Obi begins to accept bribes until the day he is caught.
Frustrated with his attempts to remain above corruption, now deeply in debt, and without the steadying influence of his mother or Clara, Obi begins to accept bribes and to have sex with prospective candidates to the Scholarship Board. He is caught accepting twenty pounds and the novel ends with everybody wondering why a young man with so much education and promise would ruin his career and his life by accepting bribes.

Booker's Seven Basic Plots Analysis: Tragedy

Anticipation Stage
Obi and Clara fall in love and Obi obtains a lucrative position with the Scholarship Board.
Obi dreams of marrying Clara. He's got a good job with the civil service and now he wants to settle down and have a family. His future is bright, and he can't wait to tell his family. He wonders why Clara isn't so eager for him to reveal her identity to his family, but he brushes it aside. He has conversations with his friends, in which he explains that there is very little temptation to be corrupt when one has a good education and has a good job prospect.

Dream Stage
Obi and Clara get engaged.

Obi soon discovers why Clara was reluctant to reveal their love: she's *osu* and it is forbidden for Obi to marry her. If he does, he'll bring shame on his family and his future children. But he doesn't care and proposes anyway. They go to buy a ring. Obi explains to his friend Joseph that he believes this is an outdated tradition that should be abolished. He will be a pioneer. Joseph cautions him, saying he thinks the time for pioneers in this matter has not yet arrived.

Frustration Stage

Mr. Mark and Elsie Mark try to offer Obi a bribe, while his finances spin out of control.

Obi soon discovers that he doesn't have a firm handle on his finances. Though he rejects the first offer of a bribe when Mr. Mark approaches him, and then again when Elise Mark offers to sleep with him, he is beginning to feel out of control financially. He borrows money from the bank to pay one bill, and accepts money from Clara to pay it back. Clara's money is stolen from his car. He receives a letter from his father, indicating that he needs to travel home as there is something important they must discuss. Obi knows they've heard news about Clara, and realizes the moment has come when he must convince them to accept her as his wife.

Nightmare Stage

Obi's family opposes his engagement and Clara has an abortion.

At home, Obi discovers that his family is unshakeable in their opposition to his marriage with Clara. His father states that Obi cannot do this, because it will bring shame on his children and his grandchildren. His mother says she would rather kill herself than see him married to an *osu.* He tries to present it in a positive light to Clara, but she knows the truth and breaks off their engagement. There is the problem of her pregnancy, however. Obi arranges for an abortion. Clara suffers an infection from the abortion procedure, and is ill in the hospital for weeks. Meanwhile, Obi discovers yet more bills that he didn't realize he would need to pay.

Destruction or Death Wish Stage

Obi's mother dies and Obi begins to accept bribes.

The last straw appears to be Obi's mother's death. Obi grieves her death but then, strangely, feels a sense of peace. After that, he begins to live the fast life. He thinks it's terrible the first time he inadvertently accepts a bribe, but then he stops feeling guilty. Soon he's caught, and found guilty in a trial where everyone wonders where he went wrong.

Three Act Plot Analysis

Act I

Obi is on trial for corruption. The judge asks how such a young, educated man, with so much promise could possibly have fallen to such lows. Though he had tried to steel himself for this moment, Obi starts to weep when he hears the judge's comment.

Act II

Obi comes home from Nigeria, having just earned his college degree. He meets Clara on the boat and begins a relationship with her. He finds a job and begins to pay back his debts to the Umuofia Progressive Union, and fulfils his duty to his parents by giving them a percentage of his monthly salary. He believes that a young educated man with a good job and good prospects for moving up the corporate and governmental ladder has little temptation to accept bribes. He learns that Clara is part of an untouchable class, the *osu*, but insists that the time has come to set those old traditions aside in favor of more modern ideas about love, marriage, and religion.

Act III

Meanwhile, Obi manages his money badly and is surprised when his annual car insurance comes due. He borrows money from the bank to pay it, then borrows money from Clara to pay the bank back. When Clara's money is stolen, Obi is now in debt to both the bank *and* his fiancée. His family asks him to return home to discuss the rumors they have heard. His father forbids his marriage to Clara, while his mother threatens to commit suicide. Obi breaks up with Clara, only to discover that she's pregnant. Her abortion puts him deeper in debt, threatens Clara's health, and ends their relationship. Obi's mother dies, and he sinks deep into a severe depression. Soon, he is accepting bribes, and earns a reputation for fulfilling his promises when bribed. He is caught accepting a twenty-pound bribe and found guilty at his trial.

Study Questions

1. Why is corruption such a big part of politics in every system in the world? Is there anything we can do to change that? Why or why not?
2. According to *No Longer At Ease*, what role did African culture play in creating the corruption in Nigeria? What role did the colonial system play in creating the corruption?
3. Consider different cultural traditions around the world that make some groups of people, or some individuals, "taboo." Do we have any "taboo" groups of people in the United States? Does your family believe some people are "taboo" because of religious, cultural, socioeconomic, racial, or other reasons?
4. What do you think about the idea of certain people groups or individuals being "taboo"? Is it a necessary part of human social systems or is it always wrong?
5. How would you compare this story to the story of *Romeo and Juliet*? How is it similar? How is it different?

Characters

All Characters

Obi Okonkwo Character Analysis

Obi's Downfall
The first chapter opens with Obi Okonkwo's trial; he is being charged with corruption and with accepting a bribe. "I cannot understand how a young man of your education and brilliant promise could have done this," the judge says (1.9). We're scratching our heads, too, and want to know. But, we have the genius, Achebe, at work. The answer to that question is what makes this story a classic tragedy.

When the plot backtracks to the period when Obi appeared to be a man of steel in his resolve to remain pure and incorruptible, we keep searching the fatal flaw that causes Obi's downfall. And guess what? It turns out to be the classic fatal flaw: hubris (excessive pride). Maybe with a bit of self-righteousness thrown into the mix. Obi has always been smarter than most of the people around him. This, combined with his isolation from Igbo culture and values, leads him to assume that he could follow his own path without consequences.

Isolation at Home and Abroad
Although his college education in England becomes the ultimate wedge that separates Obi from his cultural heritage, the isolation from his culture began at home. Even before Obi was born, his father, Isaac Okonkwo, converted to Christianity. His family adhered to Christian values with rigorous devotion, separating Obi from many aspects of his cultural heritage as an Igbo. Obi doesn't know even basic aspects of Igbo culture – such as the folk tales that other children heard from their mothers. Isaac Okonkwo's love of Western culture, religion, and especially the written word, further propelled Obi towards a Western education and achievement.

In Great Britain, Obi discovered that he longed for Nigeria. At the same time that his education trained him to look down on his traditional culture, he felt homesick for his family, friends, and home. When he met fellow Nigerians in England, he was thrilled to chat with them in Igbo. When he met an African who didn't speak Igbo and had to speak English, he felt ashamed, wondering if the people around him were judging them, as if they had no culture, no language.

This process of becoming educated was also a process of becoming increasingly alienated from his culture. Ironically, though Obi began to despise certain aspects of Igbo culture and life, he never felt comfortable or accepted in England. He thus exhibited the classic symptoms of what literary critics have called a "postcolonial identity" – feelings of discomfort in his home culture, and alienation in Western culture.

But even though Obi felt uncomfortable among the British, and realized that he'd always be considered "inferior," he became convinced of several things during his time in England. For one thing, he decided that education was the key to changing Nigeria's corrupt system, one where uneducated Nigerians were forced to use bribes to obtain jobs.

On the way home to Nigeria, he meets Clara, a beautiful nurse who was, like Obi, educated in England. Their similarities give them an instant connection. When Obi falls in love with Clara, he doesn't realize she's an *osu.* (Her identity as an *osu* means she is dedicated to a god, and Obi is supposed to shun her.) He isn't even supposed to date her, much less marry her. By the time she confesses her identity, Obi is in love and can't imagine his life without her. And so he becomes convinced that he is part of the generation that will transform harmful cultural practices. Overriding all his friends' objections, Obi and Clara get engaged. Obi overestimates his ability to convince his family to support his decision to marry someone who is taboo.

Personal and Professional Unraveling

As Obi's personal life begins to spiral out of control, so does his financial life. Obi shoulders a number of responsibilities – his parents' income during their elderly years, his brother's school fees, repayment of his scholarship – but he has failed to take account of how much it costs to maintain the lifestyle necessary for his social class. It is not that Obi is irresponsible with money, but half his salary goes to his parents or to the Umuofia Progressive Union (who gave him a scholarship for study abroad). With the half of his salary that is left over, he is supposed to own a car, keep a driver, keep a cook/servant, and maintain other expensive symbols of his elite status. At first Obi is optimistic that he can make this salary stretch, but he keeps encountering unexpected expenses, like his annual car insurance. Each unexpected expense makes Obi feel worse about his ability to shoulder the responsibilities of being a responsible man, (future) husband, and son.

When Obi's mother forbids him to marry Clara (or, rather, she says "you'll marry her over my dead body," *literally*), Obi's life takes a turn for the worse. He had optimistically hoped for the best, but he is already deeply in debt. And when he tells Clara that they need to "lay low," he discovers that she's pregnant. Obi decides that Clara needs to have an abortion, which he sees as another unexpected expense.

Though Clara understands on one level that Obi would be going against all his friends and family to marry her, she can't help but feel rejected and abandoned when Obi arranges for an abortion rather than marry her. Their relationship is already over when his mother dies. At that point, Obi begins to accept bribes. Perhaps he has grown tired of trying to remain honest when there are so few awards for it. Perhaps the two women in his life kept him more honest than he realized. What do you think?

Obi Okonkwo Timeline and Summary

- The book opens with Obi's trial.
- As he listens to the judge ask why a young man of such promise and education would do what he has done, Obi starts to cry.

- The novel flashes back to the party held in Obi's village before he left for England. His friends and family urge him to study well, and not to marry a white woman.
- Obi is homesick for Nigeria in England.
- When he returns, he is shocked by the level of poverty he sees in Lagos.
- Obi and Clara fight over going to see a film, and Obi convinces her to visit his friend Christopher.
- He and Christopher discuss the problem of corruption, and Obi expounds on his viewpoint that education provides a young man with all the skills he needs to rise to the top of his profession without relying on bribery. He believes all the men at the top, who got there because they used bribery, should be replaced with young men fresh out of college.
- The narrator flashes back to the moment when Obi and Clara meet. They first met at a dance in England, but Obi is such a poor dancer that he fails to impress Clara.
- Then he meets her again when they both move back to Nigeria and take the same boat home.
- Obi gets seasick and Clara brings him some medicine. She seems like a ministering angel.
- When the boat docks in the Madeiras, Obi and Clara disembark and spend the day together, with another passenger. When they return to the boat, Obi kisses Clara passionately and declares his love for her.
- When the boat docks, one of the officials tries to get Obi to bribe him. If Obi pays him for his radiogram, it will be only two pounds instead of five pounds tax. Obi refuses.
- Obi goes to a reception at the Umuofia Progressive Union. The reception is a huge party to welcome him home. He makes several mistakes: he wears short sleeves because it's so hot, when everybody else is dressed in a suit; and he gives a plain speech instead of a flowery, eloquent one.
- Joseph and Obi go to dinner and Obi says he'd prefer to stay with Joseph than in the hotel that the union is paying for.
- The two men reminisce about their school-days. Joseph reminds Obi that they used to call him "Dictionary," a portent sign suggesting his glorious future as one of the educated elite.
- Joseph also reminds Obi of the letter he (Obi) wrote to Hitler, and Obi admits he felt sorry for Hitler because so many people hated him.
- On the way out of the restaurant, Obi sees Clara with the Honorable Sam Okoli, an important politician.
- Soon after his return to Nigeria, Obi encounters examples of the corruption that he opposes.
- The first one happens during a job interview, when one of the interviewers asks him if he just wants the job so he can accept bribes. Obi gets angry and says that if that is why he wanted the job, it wouldn't be very prudent to say so.
- Obi and Joseph discuss marriage. Joseph says he's getting married and tells Obi that the bride-price was high, and he's uneducated with a low-paying job.
- Obi is surprised, thinking the bride-price law should have taken care of that.
- Joseph says the new law has only pushed the price higher.
- Obi jokes that it's too bad that his family won't profit from his older sisters' bride-price, since they're already married.
- Joseph says it's no joking matter, just wait until Obi sees how much he'll have to pay.
- Obi says he has no intention of paying bride-price, and Joseph says he must intend on becoming a priest then.
- Obi's second encounter with corruption occurs when he goes home to visit his family.

- When police stop the mammy wagon he's on, the driver gets angry because Obi prevents the police from just accepting a bribe rather than issuing a ticket. He says he'll never take an educated African on his wagon again.
- Obi obsesses over the fact that Clara didn't want him to tell his family about her yet. He wonders if that means she hasn't made up her mind to marry him.
- Umuofia welcomes Obi home with music and palm wine and kola nut. Hundreds of people come out for the party.
- The men tell Obi they are glad he came home "safe," meaning they are glad he didn't marry a white woman. (White women come between their African husbands and their families.) They are glad Obi didn't forget that he is a black man. Obi is proud of their approval.
- One of the men claims that Obi is the reincarnation of his grandfather, Ogbuefi Okonkwo, that they have the same spirit, the spirit that conquers the white man.
- Later that night, Obi and his father talk, and Isaac asks Obi if he had time to read the Bible in England. Obi says he did, but it was in English. He's embarrassed.
- At family prayers, Obi remembers how difficult it was for him when he was a student because his family did not observe Igbo cultural traditions.
- He was embarrassed one day in school when the teacher asked him to relate a folk tale, and he didn't know any. His mother told him the tale of a wicked leopardess who tries to eat her friend's baby lambs, but the sheep tricks the leopardess by hiding her babies inside some palm-kernels.
- Obi begins his job and discovers that his boss, Mr. Green, can be very unreasonable.
- He watches as Mr. Green tells Mr. Omo, the man that Obi is shadowing his first few days on the job, that he is paid to be obedient, not to think.
- Mr. Omo gives Obi a letter so he can purchase a car. Then he advances him money so he can buy proper clothes, as befits his new social position.
- Obi and Clara go to visit Clara's friend the Honorable Sam Okoli in his new car.
- Okoli shows Obi all his luxuries, including his radiogram with a recording machine in it. He suggests that if Obi gets tired of his job on the Scholarship Board, he might have a job for him in his Ministry.
- Obi and Clara go for a drive. Clara is clearly worried about something but doesn't want to talk about it. Obi insists.
- He reflects about how he really loves her, and he's never really loved a girl before; he always thought love was absurd.
- Finally, Clara says she cannot marry him. Obi is upset and he doesn't understand, until Clara explains: she's *osu.*
- Obi says she's being silly.
- That night, Obi tells Joseph the story. Joseph says he'd been wondering why such a beautiful girl was still unmarried. He says it's just as well Obi found out before it was too late, but Obi insists that he's going to marry her anyway.
- The next day, Obi uses his clothing allowance to buy Clara an engagement ring.
- At Clara's insistence, he also buys her a Bible, which is apparently part of the engagement custom. Then they spend the afternoon shopping.
- When he gets home, Obi tells Joseph that he's engaged to Clara now.
- Obi tries to ignore Joseph's warning, that everybody is going to be against it, and that it isn't a decision that affects just Obi and Clara, but it also will affect their children and Obi's family.

- Obi insists he's a pioneer, and Joseph says that the time for being a pioneer in marriage has not yet arrived.
- That night, Obi reflects on what Joseph said in privacy. He knows his family won't agree to it, but he thinks to himself, hopefully, that if he can just convince his mother, everything will be OK.
- Obi skips the November meeting of the Umuofia Progressive Meeting, but goes in December, arriving in his flashy new car, showing off to all the men how important he is.
- But then things sour when Obi asks for a four-month reprieve on repaying his Scholarship so he can get back on his feet.
- The President says they might be able to give him a reprieve, but they wonder if they're doing him any favors, since what he makes in one month is greater than what most of them make in an entire year.
- Further, he suggests that Obi's request may be due to the fact that he is going around with an undesirable girl.
- Obi is furious at this reference to his relationship with Clara, and he refuses the grace period they then offer on repayment.
- He has a temper tantrum, shouting that he'll start paying immediately, that second, and nothing they can do can stop him.
- Then he speeds off in his car, ignoring Joseph who tries to get him to stop.
- Mr. Mark comes to visit Obi in his office, asking him if he would do what he can to make sure his sister Elsie gets to appear before the Scholarship Board, suggesting that there's something in it for Obi if he does. Obi throws him out of his office with great pleasure.
- That afternoon, Elsie Mark visits Obi in his home, and offers to sleep with him if he'll make sure she appears before the board. He says no to her, too.
- Mr. Green had told him that he would have to pay car insurance once a year, but Obi had forgotten. Now the time has arrived, and Obi is not prepared, financially. He takes a bank draft out to pay the bill.
- Clara gets mad at Obi for thinking he couldn't ask her for help when he discovered his car insurance bill. She sends him fifty pounds the next day and tells him to cancel the bank draft.
- But Obi doesn't cancel it right away, thinking he can convince her to take the money back. She says she'll take it back but then he discovers that he'd rather owe her than the bank so he keeps the money.
- Clara and Obi go dancing that night. While they're in the nightclub, somebody enters their unlocked car and steals her fifty pounds.
- Obi receives a letter from his parents, saying that his mother is in the hospital and asking him to come home to discuss something important. Obi realizes that somebody has now told them about Clara.
- Mr. Green tells Obi that it's outrageous how educated Nigerians expect so many privileges from their jobs, such as this one young man who wants not only his own expenses paid but his girlfriend's as well.
- To get his mind off his father's letter, Obi visits Christopher.
- They discuss Elsie Mark's offer to sleep with him, and Obi is shocked that Christopher doesn't see anything wrong with accepting such a bribe.
- But no matter how much they argue, Obi can't get his mind off his father's letter.
- Before Obi leaves to go home, Clara breaks up with him. She says she doesn't want to come between Obi and his family.

- But Obi again tells her she's ridiculous and says the real reason she doesn't want to marry him is because he is bad with money.
- When he arrives home, Obi discovers that his mother is very ill, and he is sick with worry.
- Isaac discusses the news he has heard about Obi and Clara.
- When Obi tells him who Clara is, he laughs, and tells Obi that he can't marry Clara.
- Obi tries to argue that there are good reasons, rooted in Christianity, to break this taboo but is unable to convince his father.
- Obi's mother Hannah tells him that she will commit suicide if he marries Clara before she dies.
- Obi tells his father that he's going back to Lagos early.
- Isaac reminds Obi that he left his family to become a Christian, so he knows what it means to lose family, and what it means to be a Christian. It is a subtle chastisement for Obi's arguments the night before that Isaac should accept his marriage to Clara because he is a Christian.
- Obi survives a bad car accident on the way home, walking away without a bruise.
- He goes to Clara's and tells her that they just need to lay low. But he doesn't protest when Clara gives him her ring back.
- Obi visits Christopher to tell him the engagement is over.
- He asks for help because he believes Clara is pregnant, and wonders if Christopher knows of any doctors who can help him out. He asks Christopher to be discreet when he makes calls to get information.
- The first abortion doctor refuses to do it, then asks Obi why he doesn't marry Clara.
- The second doctor agrees to do it but he, too, asks Obi why he doesn't want to get married.
- Obi borrows the money for the abortion from the Hon. Sam Okoli.
- When Obi leaves Clara with the doctor, he has a split second premonition that he'll never see her again.
- Obi watches as they drive away and wonders if he should call out, "Stop! Let's get married!" But he doesn't do it.
- Only after they have driven away does he go looking, in panic, thinking he can still stop this thing.
- He returns that evening, but the doctor says he's keeping her overnight just in case something goes wrong.
- Obi asks if he can see her in the morning and the doctor says maybe, if she's willing.
- In the morning, however, he discovers that she developed complications and she's in a hospital.
- Mr. Green tells Obi that Nigerians these days have too many privileges.
-]Marie Tomlinson agrees and Obi responds that they're hypocrites, since Europeans were the ones who devised the privileges in the first place, and now they complain just because a few Africans have those privileges now.
- Obi discovers that the money he was given for his trip home was not to be spent in any way he liked. He must submit an expenditure form, accounting for each pound, and give back the remaining balance. Since he's already spent the money, this is going to be a problem, but he tries not to worry about that just yet.
- He examines the reasons why he's gotten into this mess, and decides that the reason is that he has to pay 20 pounds to the Umuofia Progressive Union every month.
- Then a messenger comes and returns the letter he had sent to Clara. Unopened.

- Obi had spent forever trying to write the short note that said he couldn't believe it was over.
- He goes to the hospital again early in the morning. But again, he doesn't see Clara.
- Obi still intends to pay Clara back her 50 pounds, but that doesn't happen. Why? Because he suddenly discovers he owes Income Tax. Marie gives him lots of good advice, a little too late: Next year, she says, have the bank take a little out each month to pay it.
- Then, if that's not bad enough, Obi's mom dies.
- Obi sends as much money as possible, but he doesn't go home for the funeral. He wonders what would be the point? She'd already be buried by the time he got there.
- But then he grieves. He goes to bed and he sleeps like he hasn't slept in *months.*
- Joseph brings beer, saying he'll need it.
- And sure enough, members of the Umuofia Progressive Union show up to be with Obi in his hour of need.
- Of course, most of the visitors are sympathetic, but at an unfortunate moment when everybody falls silent, Obi overhears one of the members telling a tale about Tortoise, who went far from home, so far that his family knew he wouldn't even return for his mother's funeral unless they told him something new and amazing had happened.
- Everybody is embarrassed when they hear the story, loosely allegorical and critical of Obi.
- Obi sleeps again all night, wondering what's wrong with himself, why he feels so much peace. He eats a ton of food when he wakes up, and criticizes himself for having an appetite.
- Then Obi remembers a story about his mother. The local priest of Udo, one of the gods of Aninta, used to let his goat wander into the Okonkwo yard, despite Isaac's requests that he keep the goat tied up. Finally, Obi's mother, Hannah, was so angry and frustrated that she just hacked the goat's head off. But nobody did anything about it because their spirits had been broken by an incident that had occurred fifteen years ago, when European soldiers had punished the men of Aninta by destroying their guns.
- Soon Obi is accepting bribes. The first time, the man just leaves the money on his coffee table. Obi puts a newspaper over it, to hide it, murmuring how terrible this is. But soon, he's complicit with it until the day he is caught.
- *No Longer At Ease* ends just as it began: everybody wonders why Obi chose the route of corruption.

Clara Okeke Character Analysis

Obi first meets Clara at a dance in England. She is so beautiful that he becomes awkward around her and continuously steps on her toes; she doesn't dance with him again. Then, by coincidence, they both take the same boat home from England to Nigeria.

As a nurse, Clara goes around administering medicine to seasick patients, and she seems like an angel to Obi. He quickly initiates a relationship. Clara is a practical girl, not to mention smart and hard working. Though she is Igbo, she is educated in the Western tradition and lives a modern lifestyle. However, Clara seems to lack the disdain Obi has for traditional culture. Every fault Obi has, Clara counter-balances.

Too Good To Be True

There has be something wrong with somebody who seems *too* perfect, right? Clara was right when she first told Obi that he didn't really love her and she would regret giving in to his flattery. Soon we discover she has a secret. Her secret is culturally specific – something only another Igbo would care about. She is an *osu*, part of a social caste forbidden to marry because one of her ancestors was dedicated to a god. They are considered taboo. As Isaac points out, marrying her would be like marrying a leper.

Once Clara admits this to Obi, she tries to break up with him. She says it's not fair to keep the relationship going; she doesn't want to come between Obi and his family. Though Clara was educated in England, and probably wonders about the justice of her taboo status, she never voices those thoughts aloud. Instead, it's clear that she understands how deeply these traditions run. She knows that Obi's parents will never accept her as a daughter-in-law, even though they are Christians and should, theoretically, disagree with a tradition like this. Clara's parents are Christians, too, but that hasn't changed their status as *osus* or the fact that they are outcasts, even in the church. Though Clara keeps trying to break up with Obi because of this fact, and Obi keeps stubbornly refusing to be broken up with, the relationship's demise is clear, at least to her. She's just sorry, in the end, that she didn't do something about it before she ended up pregnant. That is what makes her bitter.

Clara Sees the End Is Near

When Obi returns from his family's house after breaking the news that he is engaged to an *osu*, Clara understands that their relationship is over, even though Obi only tells her that they should lay low for a while. She could handle the breakup when she knew it was about family, but after the abortion, she isn't interested in seeing Obi ever again.

Though Clara allows Obi to arrange the abortion for her, it's not clear if she wants to go through with it. However, it's obvious that she doesn't forgive him for it. When the doctor suggests that they get married instead, Clara says, sullenly, "I don't want to marry him" (15.50). By then, she's figured out or decided that Obi is not a great guy. The abortion goes badly and Clara spends weeks in the hospital recovering. Though Obi tries to get back together with her, sending her a note saying they can work this out, Clara returns the note unopened.

Clara Okeke Timeline and Summary

- Clara and Obi fight over going to see a film, and Clara accompanies Obi to his friend Christopher's house.
- The book flashes back to Clara and Obi's first meeting. Clara is unimpressed with Obi's dancing skills, and limps off after he crushes her feet.
- Clara doesn't recognize Obi when she meets him again on the boat to Nigeria after they have both graduated.
- She brings medicine to all the passengers who are seasick. She's a nurse, after all, but somehow it makes Obi think she's has feelings for him. Or it makes him have feelings for

her.

- When Obi declares his love for Clara, she tells him he's being silly and will forget about him by morning. Then she kisses him.
- Months later, Obi and Clara's relationship is established.
- The night Obi gets a car, the two go for a drive. Clara is clearly worried about something but doesn't want to talk about it.
- Obi insists. He reflects about how he really loves her, and he's never really loved a girl before –always thought it was absurd, in fact.
- Finally, Clara says she cannot marry him. Obi is upset and he doesn't understand, until Clara explains: she's *osu.*
- Obi insists they can get married anyway.
- The next day, Obi uses his clothing allowance to buy Clara an engagement ring.
- At Clara's insistence, he also buys her a Bible, which is apparently part of the engagement custom. Then they spend the afternoon shopping.
- Clara comes home when Elise Mark is there, just after Elise has offered to sleep with Obi if he can get her an appearance before the Board.
- Clara's a pretty cool cookie. She doesn't blink an eyelash, seeing another woman in her fiancée's apartment. But she does apologize later for spoiling his good time.
- After she hears the story, she tells Obi that he was too hard on Mr. Mark. Her reasoning is that offering money is not as bad as offering your body.
- Clara gets mad at Obi for thinking he couldn't ask her for help when he discovered his car insurance bill.
- She sends him fifty pounds the next day and tells him to cancel the bank draft.
- She and Obi go dancing that night.
- While they're in the nightclub, somebody enters their unlocked car and steals her fifty pounds.
- Clara breaks up with Obi so that she doesn't come between Obi and his family.
- Obi coaxes her back to him by claiming that the real reason she doesn't want to marry him is because he's bad with money.
- When Obi returns and says they need to just lay low for a while, Clara knows what he really means.
- She gives Obi his ring back and says there is something else, but she'll figure out a way to take care of it.
- At the abortion doctor's office, the doctor asks Obi why he doesn't marry Clara. Clara says she has no interest in marrying Obi.
- Clara's abortion turns septic and she ends up in the hospital.
- Clara returns Obi's letter of apology to him, unopened.
- Clara leaves Lagos when she gets out of the hospital.

Isaac Okonkwo Character Analysis

Anybody who read *Things Fall Apart* will recognize Isaac Okonkwo (called Nwoye before he converted to Christianity). As a young man, he left his father's house and became a Christian, severing his ties with his family and his heritage. As an older man, we see where that path has led him.

Isaac's love for the written word brings glory to his family when his son Obi proves to be brilliant and becomes the top pick to go to Great Britain for college. But despite his lifelong devotion to the church and his work as a catechist, Isaac Okonkwo has very little money in his old age, and he is dependent on his son. This doesn't make Isaac weak, however. He still has an opinion. And he surprises his son because, despite his adherence to Christianity and his love for the written word, there are parts of his culture heritage for he has great respect. He refuses to be convinced that Obi's engagement to Clara is a good idea. Using his patriarchal authority, he tells Obi simply that he cannot marry her.

And he does not budge. In our last glimpse of Isaac in this novel, he explains to Obi that he knows better than anyone what it means to be a Christian, and Obi cannot tell him that it is a Christian act to marry an *osu*. That reminder has a double importance, though. Isaac is also reminding his son that when he has decided something, when he has set his mind on a path, he does not give up. He is determined. Obi is either willfully blind, wishful, or simply lying when he tells Clara that his father will come around. The truth is, Isaac is just as stubborn now as he was the day he left his father's house and joined the Christians. His will is iron. He will not bend.

Isaac Okonkwo Timeline and Summary

- Isaac Okonkwo has a religious discussion with some of the merry-makers celebrating the return of Obi after four years in England.
- Isaac claims that rainmaking ceremonies are useless, and that rainmakers do not have the power to prevent lightning from striking people. He says that it is the work of God that no person in Umuofia has been killed by lightning. (The word for thunder exists in Igbo, so it's hard to know if Achebe was making a joke here or if he just used the wrong word.)
- The merry-makers want to break a kola nut, but Isaac insists they use kola nut that hasn't been sacrificed to idols since his is a Christian house.
- When one of the men claims that Obi is the reincarnation of his grandfather, Isaac claims that dead men do not return.
- Obi and his father talk, and Isaac asks Obi if he had time to read the Bible in England. Obi says he did, but it was in English.
- When Obi returns for a visit at Isaac's request, Isaac is clearly dismayed that Obi is dating an *osu*.
- Isaac says Obi doesn't realize the depth of what he wants to do, and that he will be bringing a curse upon his family, and upon his children.
- Isaac listens to Obi's arguments but tells him that *osu* is like leprosy. You can marry a leper, but you can't expect people to agree to it. The stigma is too strong.
- The next day, Isaac reminds Obi of all that he had given up in order to become a Christian. He explains that his father cursed him, which is a terrible thing to do to a child. He tells Obi that because he went through fire to be a Christian, he understands what it means to be a Christian more than Obi ever can.

Hannah Okonkwo Character Analysis

Hannah Okonkwo is Obi's mother. She is obedient to her husband Isaac's decree that they forsake certain Igbo traditions because of their Christian beliefs. But it is also clear that Hannah still respects Igbo culture and many traditions. There is a telling moment in the text when the narrator describes how the European custom of cutting the cake at a wedding had been reinterpreted in Igbo culture. The idea was that the person who cuts the cake first will be the senior partner. The day that Isaac and Hannah were married, Hannah cut the cake first.

Though Hannah and Isaac keep their children from most parts of Igbo culture, Hannah was willing to secretly break her husband's decree when she realized that Obi was suffering at school because he had no knowledge of Igbo folk tales. We see further evidence of Hannah's adherence to certain cultural customs the day she calls Obi to her bedside and explains that if he marries Clara, she will kill herself. This is Obi's last interaction with Hannah. She dies shortly thereafter.

Hannah Okonkwo Timeline and Summary

- Obi's mother has grown quite ill during the time he was in England, and her obvious bad health makes Obi feel bad.
- Obi remembers how his mother tried to honor Obi's father's beliefs by leaving much of Igbo culture behind.
- But at least once, she disobeyed Isaac's wishes.. After Obi's classmates made fun of him for not knowing any Igbo folk-tales, she told him one tale so he wouldn't be embarrassed at school.
- When Obi becomes engaged, secretly, to Clara, he knows his family will be against it. But he thinks about the special bond he has with his mother.
- One memory stands out: the time she cut her hand badly with a razor blade that he used to sharpen his pencils. The fact that she had shed her blood for him always connected him to her in a special way. He is certain that if he can just convince his mother to accept Clara, everything will be OK.
- Obi's mother, ill and dying, tells him that if he marries Clara before she dies, her blood will be on his head because she will kill herself. But he can do what he likes once she is dead and that is likely to be soon.
- Hannah Okonkwo dies.
- After his mother has passed away, Obi remembers a story about his mother.
- The local priest of Udo, one of the gods of Aninta, used to let his goat wander into the Okonkwo yard, despite Isaac's requests that he keep the goat tied up. Finally, Hannah was so angry and frustrated that she just hacked the goat's head off. But nobody did anything about it because their spirits had been broken by an incident that had occurred fifteen years ago, when European soldiers had punished the men of Aninta by destroying their guns.

Joseph Okeke Character Analysis

Joseph is Obi's friend and kinsmen. He shows Obi the ropes in Lagos before he leaves for Nigeria, then shows Obi the ropes again when he returns. Though Joseph may not be educated, he does understand his culture, and he tries to gently guide Obi on a path that will be mutually beneficial to everyone in Obi's life. Even though Obi abandons Joseph when he criticizes his decision to marry Clara, Joseph remains a faithful friend. After Hannah Okonkwo's death, Joseph brings beer to Obi's apartment so that Obi can offer the traditional libation to the friends and family who come to mourn his mother's death. Joseph proves to be a faithful, wise friend.

Joseph Okeke Timeline and Summary

- When Obi stays in Lagos on his way to England, Joseph tells him about his many girlfriends. He brings a woman home for the night, and kicks Obi out until he's done pleasuring her.
- When Obi returns from England, Joseph is pleased that Obi wants to stay with him instead of at a hotel.
- Obi and Joseph discuss marriage. Joseph says he's getting married and tells Obi that the bride-price was high, and he's uneducated with a low-paying job.
- Obi is surprised, thinking the bride-price law should have taken care of that. Joseph says the new law has only pushed the price higher.
- Obi jokes that it's too bad that his family won't profit from his older sisters' bride-prices since they're already married.
- Joseph says it's no joking matter, Obi will have to pay even more than he does.
- Obi says he has no intention of paying bride-price, and Joseph says he must intend on becoming a priest then.
- Joseph is shocked when Obi insists that he's going to marry Clara, even though she's *osu*. He says Obi must not understand the nature of the taboo, or how strong a tradition it is.
- The next day, when Obi tells Joseph that he is now engaged to Clara, Joseph asks if he plans to get married the English way or the traditional way. Obi says he hasn't yet decided.
- Joseph tries to warn him that he will not receive approval from his family, that it also affects future generations including Obi's children.
- Obi insists he's a pioneer, and Joseph says that the time for being a pioneer in marriage has not yet arrived.
- Obi brings Joseph to the December meeting of the Umuofia Progressive Union in his brand-new flashy car. It makes him feel proud.
- Joseph tries to convince Obi not to rush off in a rage after the President of the Union suggested that his relationship with Clara was inappropriate.
- Joseph brings bottles of beer over to Obi's house, saying that he'll need them for the

people who come to mourn his mother's death.

Christopher Character Analysis

Christopher is another one of Obi's friends. We don't know much about Christopher except that he loves women and partying. He provides a contrast to Obi because he finds it completely acceptable that women should use their bodies to bribe men in power (such as Obi) to give them favors. Even though Christopher seems thoroughly untraditional, in the end Christopher also adheres to traditional Igbo culture, and criticizes Obi's decision to pursue Clara. Unlike Joseph, however, Christopher waits until the relationship is over before he tells Obi what he really thinks.

Christopher Timeline and Summary

- Obi and Christopher discuss corruption and Christopher argues that just because a person is educated doesn't make them more qualified for a job. Experience is important too.
- Christopher takes one of his girlfriends, Bisi, dancing with Obi and Clara on the night the money is stolen from Obi's car.
- Obi and Christopher go to visit two Irish girls that they had met and sometimes played tennis with. But the girls have discovered that it's not OK for them to go around with African men so they leave quickly.
- Christopher tells Obi that there was no reason why he shouldn't have slept with Elsie Mark. If Elsie was going to appear before the Scholarship Board anyway, then it was not a conflict of interest for Obi to sleep with her if she offered.
- Christopher argues that it's worse to take money from somebody, because they'll actually miss that.
- Christopher tells Obi he always thought his relationship with Clara was a bad thing, but he knew better than to interfere with a man when he is in love.
- Christopher agrees to find an abortion doctor for Obi, so he can take care of Clara's pregnancy.

Mr. William Green Character Analysis

Mr. Green, a civil servant, is something of a contradiction. On the one hand, he doesn't seem to think much of modern Nigeria or modern Africans. Obi thinks that Mr. Green works incredibly hard for something he doesn't even believe in. Mr. Green seems to be a tragic figure: somebody who works desperately for a country, believing in an idealized Africa that will never exist.

Mr. Green probably doesn't know what Obi thinks. In fact Mr. Green seems like the kind of boss who would take offense at Obi's assessment of him. After all, he's the one who tells Obi that if he has half a brain and isn't lazy, he'll do all-right, and then turns around and tells his African Administrative Assistant that he's there to do what he's told, not to think. Mr. Green follows this up by barking at Obi to refer to him as "sir" since he is, after all, Obi's senior. Mr. Green is certain of one thing: all Africans are corrupt. But the narrator notes that, in the end, not even Mr. Green understands *why* Africans like Obi are corrupt.

Mr. William Green Timeline and Summary

- Taking a break from Obi Okonkwo's trial, Mr. Green explains to his tennis partner that all Africans are corrupt and this is why African countries should never achieve self-rule.
- The novel flashes back in time so we next see Mr. Green on Obi's first day on the job.
- Mr. Green tells Obi that if he's not lazy and if he's prepared to use his brain, he'll do fine.
- Then Mr. Green tells Mr. Omo, the Administrative Assistant, that he is paid to be obedient, not to use his brain.
- Later, when Mr. Green calls Obi to ask him a question, he rebukes Obi for failing to call him "sir."
- Mr. Green had told Obi when he first started working that he would have to pay car insurance once a year, but Obi forgets.
- Mr. Green tells Obi that it's outrageous how educated Nigerians expect so many privileges from their jobs, such as this one young man who wants not only his own expenses paid but his girlfriend's as well.
- Mr. Green criticizes Obi's decision to go on local leave. He claims that this is a perk that was intended for Europeans to leave hot, humid, muggy Lagos to get to a cooler climate. He believes that Nigerians, who go on leave, are abusing their privileges.

Marie Tomlinson Character Analysis

Marie Tomlinson is Mr. Green's secretary. Young, pretty, and European, Marie becomes friends with Obi by criticizing Mr. Green and praising Clara. Obi succumbs to the flattery. Yet, though Marie denigrates Mr. Green, she reveals that she thinks he has a point when he suggests that educated Nigerians expect too many luxuries and privileges from a senior civil servant position. She doesn't seem to recognize the hypocrisy in her criticism. The privileges were originally created for Europeans who held the positions, and now Europeans are complaining that Africans who hold those same positions shouldn't have the same privileges.

Marie Tomlinson Timeline and Summary

- Marie asks Obi if Mr. Green seems odd.
- Obi is suspicious of Marie's motivation, but when Marie tells him how lovely Clara is, and

seems genuinely excited about their engagement, he lets down his guard.
- Marie is curious about why Mr. Mark came to visit Obi, but Obi doesn't tell her why.
- Soon Marie and Obi are on the best of terms and are even calling each other by their first names.
- Marie agrees with Mr. Green when he criticizes Nigerians for taking too much vacation time, and for having too many holidays. She says she would never get as many holidays in Great Britain as Africans expect in Nigeria.
- When Obi argues with her, she tells him he doesn't look well, and suggests he take something for malaria, then go see a doctor.

Character Roles

Protagonist
Obi Okonkwo
Obi is more of an anti-hero than a classic hero. Though sympathize with him and want him to succeed, the truth is that his goals are not goals we can support. Of course we want him to succeed in refraining from corruption, but we know from the beginning that he fails. So instead, we are constantly aware of all the aspects of his character that lead to his downfall – his pride, his self-righteousness, his flawed reasoning, his stubbornness, and the way he holds onto love (and Clara) even though every friend and family member and, indeed, Clara herself tell him to let go.

Antagonist
Mr. Green
Mr. Green genuinely loves Africa, but he dreams of the "old" Africa during the colonial era, when Europeans had total power and could shape the destiny of the nation. He continually makes cutting comments about Africans, criticizing their inherent laziness, their consistent corruption, and their willingness to make unrealistic demands.

Antagonist
Umuofia Progressive Union, Igbo versus Western Values, Familial Pressures
This is quite a mouthful, and it might not be fair to group all of these separate forces into one category of antagonism, but just consider how all of the above affect Obi and contribute to his downfall. These three significant forces together hold Obi to impossible standards. And since he is the first young Igbo man to be in this position, there is no precedent which helps guide him. You could argue that the combination of these pressures puts Obi into an impossibly situation. He lacks the ability to deal responsibly and appropriately with this multitude of pressures, and seems to be unwilling to ask for help.

Guide/Mentor
Joseph
Joseph understands Igbo culture. He helps Obi adjust back into Nigerian life, supports him in his attempt to remain free of corruption, and cautions him against dating Clara. Though Obi cuts off

contact with Joseph after he criticizes Obi's engagement to Clara, Joseph returns to help Obi after Hannah Okonkwo's death, bringing the necessary bottles of beer, the customary offering to those who come to grieve with you.

Foil

Christopher

Like Obi, Christopher is educated, but unlike Obi, Christopher still embraces his Igbo culture. He says nothing until Obi's engagement with Clara is over, but then he says that it is for the best: he would never marry an *osu*.

Romantic Interest

Clara

Clara is lovely, educated, and practical. She possesses all the qualities that Obi *needs* in his life, and he recognizes that. But Clara knows better than Obi that her identity as an *osu* makes their marriage impossible. Against her better judgment, she accepts his marriage proposal, but continuously tries to break the relationship off, saying it's for his own good.

Character Clues

Names

Obi's nickname during school was "Dictionary" because of his school smarts. This is an early indication of the way Obi relies and falls back on the written word, something that is reflected later when he becomes known as a member of the community who has learned "book." Isolated from his cultural heritage due to his father's Christianity, Obi embraces Western education and becomes even further alienated from his kinsmen.

Obi's full name is Obiajuli, which means "the mind at last is at rest." When translated, this is actually a characterization of Obi's father, Isaac, who had been anxious because his wife gave birth to four daughters before she finally gave birth to one son. This given name reveals the importance of having a son, and how men in Igbo culture are emasculated if they have nothing but daughters. His name is also ironic, since Obi's mind is never at rest; he is ceaselessly thinking about the problems of Nigeria, the problems of independence, the problems involved in getting his parents to agree to his marriage to Clara. As the title of the book clearly indicates, he is "no longer at ease."

Other names in the book indicate the influence of Western values and culture. Clara's name is an English name, indicating her family's support for the ways of the West. We also are made aware of her family's westernization because they must have supported her to study medicine in England. Both the fact that she studied Western medicine (rather than traditional healing), and the fact that she studied it in a western country, is further evidence of the westernization of her family's values.

We know that Isaac Okonkwo took a new name when he became a Christian. His original name, which we know from *Things Fall Apart*, was called Nwoye. His new name suggests that Isaac cast off his past identity and assumed a new identity, one affiliated with a Western religion and Western ideals.

Education

Obi's education in a Western system alienates him from the customs of his family and his kinsmen. He fails to understand how deeply certain cultural values are held, even by his Christian family members, and violates taboos by becoming involved with Clara. But his pride – helped by the fact that his education and income level is superior to everyone he knows –prevents him from seeing how destructive his stubbornness will prove to be.

Obi's western education, like Clara's education, sets him apart from his friends and family. He has different values and different ideas about how life should be lived and the government should be run. But there are also other kinds of education. We see that Joseph, who only finished part of his schooling and never went to college, is far more educated in the ways of Igbo life. He understands how things should be done, how Obi should behave, and where it is acceptable to push the boundaries of Igbo values. He is educated in a different way and has cultural smarts that Obi lacks.

Though Isaac Okonkwo never went to college, he was educated and trained in the ways of the Christian church and became a catechist. He is complicit with trying to re-orient Igbo culture away from traditional values and towards the values of a new religion. As a character, it suggests that Isaac is firmly attached to the new identity he has assumed as a Christian, and he is willing to reject many parts of his old identity in order to fit into the new religion.

Family Life

Obi's family life is characterized by a dual value system. On the one hand, his father holds firmly to western literacy and religious ideals as his guiding light; he shields his children from aspects of Igbo culture that he sees as destructive and superstitious. Obi's mother, alternatively, is outwardly submissive to her husband's religion and value-system, but she nevertheless clings to her culture and traditions. In certain subversive moments, she tries to teach her children to respect Igbo culture, such as when she teaches Obi Igbo folk tales so he can relate them in school. This dual value system creates conflict and tension within Obi as he pursues goals that were conceived within and perpetuated by western educational, religious, and business values.

Literary Devices

Symbols, Imagery, Allegory

The Written Word

The written word symbolizes the power of Europeans, which Achebe tells us outright. We see that Isaac Okonkwo embraces it early on:

Mr. Okonkwo believed utterly and completely in the things of the white man. And the symbol of the white man's power was the written word, or better still, the printed word... (13.24).

It isn't just the two Okonkwos who recognize the power of the written word. The Umuofia Progressive Union is made up of poorly educated men who recognized the power of knowing "book," and who saved their pennies scrupulously to send one of their "sons" to England to go to college. They knew that having an educated kinsmen would give them access to the upper echelons of power within Nigeria.

Both Obi Okonkwo and his father Isaac embrace the written word as part of their identity. As a result, both seem to identify with European values and culture, at the expense of their own people. Obi becomes engaged in a life-long pursuit of European power by relying on his literacy. He soon realizes, however, that is not enough. Disengaged from the traditions of his people, he nevertheless gets caught up in the corrupt African power system that involves bribery. However, and perhaps because of his life-long pursuit of the written word, he lacks the street smarts to be effective in his corruption. In an ironic turn of events, he is soon caught and sentenced in a European court system, by European values, which he had adopted by embracing the written word.

Obi's Razor and Pencils

Obi remembers how his mother cut herself on his razor while washing his clothes. Obi had used the razor to sharpen his pencils for school. The pencils, newly introduced to Igbo culture with the advent of churches and schools, symbolize the intrusion of western ideals and ways of life into rural Igbo villages. This symbolically foreshadows the way that Obi later wounds his mother by utterly abandoning the traditions and culture of the Igbo, and embracing instead western values and principles. Obi's abandonment of his native culture seems inevitable given the fact that Obi left home to be educated in Europe and returns to occupy a European civil servant post in a westernized part of Lagos.

Mr. Green

Mr. Green symbolizes the colonial mentality, which recognizes that some Africans may be intelligent but believes that African culture is inherently inferior to European culture. Furthermore, Mr. Green believes that no African can ever escape the "curse" of his culture, and will eventually succumb to the temptations of corruption and laziness.

The Umuofia Progressive Union

The Umuofia Progressive Union symbolizes a body of African men intent on hanging onto their indigenous culture even while succeeding in the new world of capitalism, business, and Western values. What is interesting is that values that succeeded and worked well in indigenous culture – like helping family members, and using different forms of currency to oil the engines of society and politics – create all sorts of problems when applied to a imposed system of Western-style business and bureaucratic government.

Hannah Okonkwo's Dream

Hannah Okonkwo dreams that termites eat the bed underneath her. She realizes that Obi's westernized values are leaving her with nothing solid beneath her; they are eating up the very thing that supports her, her cultural values.

Setting

Lagos, Nigeria and Umuofia, Nigeria in the 1950s
No Longer At Ease is set in the 1950s, before Nigeria achieved independence from Great Britain. Though the British had been trading in Nigeria and had sent numerous missionaries to convert the region during the 18th century, they took possession of Nigeria by force in the late 19th century, from about 1885-1900. This violent period was known, ironically, as the "pacification" of Nigeria. It was half a century before the Nigerians recovered and insisted that they had the right to self-governance. Nigeria achieved independence in 1960, a few years after the period in which the events of this book place.

More specifically, this book is set in Lagos, with a couple of brief excursions to Obi's birthplace, Umuofia. Lagos is a bustling big city and the capital of Nigeria. Lagos is where the masses of urbanites live – both African and European – in generally segregated neighborhoods. By the 1950s, however, some educated Africans with senior positions, such as Obi, live in the European quarters because they can afford to escape the squalor and poverty found in most of the African neighborhoods.

Umuofia is an umbrella term that describes a collection of villages in rural Igbo, in the southern part of Nigeria. The rural villagers live a very different life than those Africans in the city. Though cultural and religious traditions have changed dramatically since the pacification period, the rural villagers retain more of their respect for traditional customs than those Africans in the city who are busy acquiring western values.

By contrasting city life with village life, Achebe achieves a couple of important things. First of all, he shows how modernity and urban lifestyles erode traditional culture. We also observe more poverty in the city, since the people who live in the city lack the safety nets provided by traditional culture and customs that exist in the rural areas. As Obi observed when he went with Clara to her seamstress, who lived in a seedier part of the city:

His car was parked close to a wide-open storm drain from which came a very strong smell of rotting flesh. It was the remains of a dog which had no doubt been run over by a taxi....Here was Lagos, though Obi the real Lagos he hadn't imagined existed until now . (2.14, 17)

In addition to showing the destruction caused by urban life, we are able to see that village life has its own problems. Though the people there might not experience the same destitution and squalor, they recognize that the future will not look anything like what they knew in the past. This is why they tax themselves mercilessly to send their young people to get college education. The villagers know that it is only a matter of time before their way of life is gone forever, and in the meantime, they must work hard to plan for a different future.

One of the interesting aspects of Achebe's comparison between village and city life, however, is the recognition that some cultural concepts and traditions are entrenched deeply, no matter where you go. Clara's identity as an *osu* is one example. Though Obi and many of his kinsmen live in the "new" Nigeria – the modern world of cars and politics and dating – they are unwilling to let go of their ancient taboos. These follow them to the city.

Narrator Point of View

Third Person (Limited Omniscient)
This book is told in the third person, looking in from the outside on Obi's life, habits, and thoughts. We are not privy to other people's ideas or thoughts, unless they express them to Obi. This narrative technique allows us to inspect Obi's life and thoughts from a distance, analyzing them for discrepancies. At the same time, we get to see his choices and ideas close enough to feel sympathy. We recognize that Obi is a man caught between two different worlds as society around him is rapidly transformed. The next generation will not feel the same sense of alienation he feels. The third person limited omniscient allows us both to observe Obi's contradictory behavior, while feeling sympathy for his situation.

Genre

Tragedy
No Longer At Ease is a classic tragedy. A classic tragedy is the story of a man or woman who tries to change the world. In the end, their pride is the fatal flaw and they end up destroying themselves or becoming part of the system they had meant to destroy.

In *No Longer At Ease*, Obi Okonkwo, the protagonist, is optimistic and believes in his own power, and the power of young Western-educated people to change Nigeria. As a result of his optimism, he pits his idealism against the mighty system of corruption and bribery that dominates the inner workings of Nigerian government and business. He also pits his belief in the superiority of western values against his culture's traditions.

In both cases, Obi is the loser. His hubris (excessive pride) is so great that he is unable to consider the gentle criticisms that friends and family offer him as they try to steer him on a path that will allow him to live successfully in a new society. Blinded by his own belief in his ability to change the world, or at least the world of Nigerian politics and culture, he keeps heading down the path that leads to his demise.

Ultimately, Obi is unable to convince his family to accept Clara as his future wife, and he eventually succumbs to the temptation of accepting bribes.

Tone

Detached, Scientific
In the third paragraph of *No Longer At Ease*, the judge assigned to Obi Okonkwo's case

regards Obi the way a "collector fixes his insect with formalin" (1.3). The omniscient narrator in *No Longer At Ease* is no more sympathetic to Obi than this judge. The tone is coldly analytical, almost scientific in its precision, demonstrating in step-by-step fashion just how Obi deserted his lofty principles and started to accept bribes. Consider the following example:

Obi's theory that the public service of Nigeria would remain corrupt until the old Africans at the top were replaced by young men from the universities was first formulated in a paper read to the Nigerian Students' Union in London. But unlike most theories formed by students in London, this one survived the first impact of homecoming (5.1).

These two sentences reveal Obi's theories from an incredible distance, allowing us to analyze how African students who study abroad might form criticisms of their home country, generally speaking. At the same time, these two sentences provide us with some sympathy for Obi. After all, who wouldn't applaud Obi's attempts to reform a corrupt system, even if those attempts are merely writing a student paper while in college? Though the tone allows us to feel sympathy for Obi, recognizing the pressures that surround him, it also enables us to dissect and understand the impulses and influences that ultimately lead to his demise.

Writing Style

Plain, Straightforward

Achebe's writing style lacks frills, flowery-speech, and excessive metaphors or symbols. For example, in following passage, Achebe is straight-forward in his description of Obi's thought patterns:

Obi felt very sorry for her. She was obviously an intelligent girl who had set her mind, like so man other young Nigerians, on university education. And who could blame them? Certainly not Obi. It was rather sheer hypocrisy to ask if a scholarship was as important as all that or if university education was worth it. Every Nigerian knew the answer. It was yes (9.72).

In this passage, we are deep inside Obi's head, yet this brief explanation provides everything we need to know about why bribery and corruption was so wide-spread in Nigerian society: when corruption is the one path to get what you want, and when what you want is so lucrative, this kind of corruption will always be rampant.

What's Up With the Title?

In one sense, the title suggests something pretty obvious – someone once felt comfortable and is now feeling uneasy. And actually, once you get into the novel, you find out that this quick assessment is accurate. The title reflects the discomfort felt by the main character, Obi Okonkwo. His university education in England has left him feeling alienated from his family and friends. While in England, he was alone in a foreign place, thousands of miles from his family, speaking a foreign tongue. And besides all that, he comes from a warm, tropical place, and needs to adjust to living in cold, foggy, rainy England. Obi can no longer get his mother's pounded *foo-foo*, yam, or fish soup. Instead, he's had to adjust to eating boiled potatoes, boiled meat, boiled vegetables.

But that's not exactly Obi's problem. It gets a little more complicated than that.

The problem of homesickness is compounded by the fact that Obi partly rejected his own culture, embracing Western values through his Western education. As a result of his Christian upbringing (see our "Character Analysis" of Obi's father, Isaac for more on this), and his British education, Obi decided that the written word is the way to go. He suddenly found himself believing in democracy and thinking that if you want to get ahead in the world, you need to be a Christian, read and write proper English, and behave like a European.

So Obi tried. But that doesn't mean he felt comfortable in England. There he was, studying in an alien culture, feeling uncomfortable and different. However, when he returns to Nigeria, not only does he not fit in with his fellow countrymen, but he's also uncomfortable among the English expatriates in Nigeria, even though they all work together and they're supposed to be buddies. So, he doesn't feel comfortable with his own folks and he doesn't feel comfortable with the other guys, either.

Obi's estrangement from his culture is the same problem that thousands of young people in Africa and India faced after their Western educations. They are at odds with their own culture, but at the same time they are at odds with the new culture that they had (partly) embraced. On the one hand, they saw all sorts of problems with the culture they had left behind; on the other hand, they weren't accepted by the Western culture they had tried to embrace.

This is a phenomenon explored by many postcolonial writers. Colonial powers expended a great deal of effort and energy towards distinguishing between Western culture and colonized cultures; Western literature, philosophy, and popular culture portrayed colonized cultures as "inferior." Young people from colonized countries felt estranged from their own culture after their Western education, even while they were not accepted by Westerners. This condition has been called a "postcolonial identity" and Obi exhibits a classic case of it.

(If you're interested in learning more about postcolonial identity, we recommend you check out Albert Memmi's *The Colonizer and the Colonized*, Edward Said's *Orientalism*, and Gayatri Spivak's " Can the Subaltern Speak?")

What's Up with the Epigraph?

We returned to our places, these Kingdoms,
But no longer at ease here, in the old dispensation,
With an alien people clutching their gods.
I should be glad of another death.
– T.S. Eliot, "The Journey of the Magi"

The title for the novel comes from this selection of verses by T.S. Eliot, an early 20th-century American expatriate poet who eventually became a naturalized British citizen. T. S. Eliot lived in

Great Britain throughout the period when the British tried to consolidate and strengthen their hold on their colonial possessions. He was still living in Great Britain when the nation relinquished it's hold and allowed the colonies to, one by one, gain independence.

So why would Achebe pick the poem of a white man from Great Britain as the epigraph to a book that explores the postcolonial complications?

The choice of this poem, "The Journey of the Magi," is pretty brilliant. If you look at the entire poem, you realize that it's a poem about how spiritual birth can feel like death. Even though you are being born into something new, you are still witnessing the death of your old way of life, and your old beliefs. This process can be painful.

"The Journey of the Magi" details the journey of the Biblical magi (or "wise men") as they searched for Christ. The three magi saw a brilliant new star in the east and realized it signaled the birth of a new king. They followed it until they found Jesus, and they worshipped him as their king.

In Eliot's poem, the speaker talks about how the journey was difficult: it was bitterly cold and there were many times they regretted it. They had all these memories of home, where they enjoyed warm weather and "silken girls bringing sherbet." When they finally reached their destination, a humble tavern and a stable where Jesus is born, they wondered whether their journey was for a birth or a death. They had met the Messiah and though this meeting was a birth, it was a bitter birth, one more like death than birth. In the verses excerpted here, the speaker has returned to his own home, but now that he has met Christ, he is "no longer at ease" in his old culture with his old religion and his old way of life. The speaker would be glad for "another death" like the one he just experienced, perhaps because then he would feel at ease again in his old life with his family and friends.

These short verses, the final verses of the poem, describe what many writers and literary critics have called the postcolonial condition. The journey that the magi took parallels Obi Okonkwo's journey from his home to England, where he experiences an intellectual and cultural birth that is more like death. When he returns to his home country, Nigeria, he feels culturally displaced. He is "no longer at ease" among his countrymen, with their religion and their way of life. Not only does Obi judge their lack of education (and their use of bribes to climb the corporate and government ladder), but he also feels many of their other customs are barbaric and should be eradicated as citizens embrace Christianity and/or Western education.

What's Up with the Ending?

Because the beginning of *No Longer At Ease* has already provided us with the knowledge that Obi Okonkwo is guilty of corruption and accepting bribes, the actual ending of the novel is ironic. Achebe chooses not to belabor or repeat the scene in the courtroom where we learn of Obi's guilt. Instead, he ends with just a few sentences explaining that nobody knows why Obi began to accept bribes, or how he became corrupt.

We are left with a number of unsettling questions. How could Obi's family not know about his corruption? How could his parents, who willingly accepted Obi's monthly monetary gifts, not know they were part of the problem? How could his mother not know that threatening to kill herself would somehow affect him? How could the Umuofia Progressive Union not know that Obi's repayment of his debt would sometimes be difficult, more difficult than he could bear? How could they not see the stresses and strains Obi endured as he tried to become part of a class of society that he knew nothing about and could not understand? And given that bribery permeated their community, why would they assume their son to be immune?

Throughout the novel, we observe that the other people in Obi's life are complicit in his downfall. It's true that his corruption is ultimately due to his own hubris, but it's also clear that all the different people in his life play a role – from his relatives who wouldn't let him love the girl of his choice and who taxed him heavily in order to pay back his debt, to his peers in the government who demanded that he conform to a particular social lifestyle even though he couldn't financially afford it, to cultural expectations that he help his little brother through school and support his parents in their old age.

Even if everybody else pretends they're ignorant, *we* know the truth. They were *all* part of the reason why Obi became corrupt. If the beginning of the novel leaves us curious about how Obi becomes a corrupt politician, the ending points out that it is not an easy answer, possibly suggesting that our individual actions are heavily influenced by the situations we find ourselves in, the people who surround us, and the choices that others make, as well as our own.

Did You Know?

Trivia

- Achebe is the most widely read author from the African continent. His books have been translated into 40 languages. (Source)
- The kola nut is a symbol of Igbo hospitality. It is offered to visitors and guests at weddings. It contains caffeine and was once used in Coca-Cola and other soft drinks. It is now used in Red Bull's Simply Cola. Kola nut is pretty bitter and takes getting used to – kind of like coffee. It has been used to treat whooping cough and asthma, apparently opens up the bronchial tubes as a result of the caffeine. (Source)
- Achebe wrote his novels in English. Though this may seem like a reasonable choice, it had huge political implications and he was criticized for it by other African novelists. African novelist Ngugi wa Thiong'o wrote in his native tongue, Gikuyu, in part because he was rejecting the language of the colonizer. (Ngugi also got thrown into prison for it because it was seen as resistance to the government.) Ngugi claimed that to write in the language of the colonizer is to acquiesce to your own domination. The language of the colonizer was always a politically sensitive issue, as evidenced by the Soweto riots in South Africa in 1977, when schoolchildren boycotted schools because they no longer wanted to be educated in the language of the oppressor. Though Achebe was criticized for it, he chose to write in English because he recognized that it was a language that allowed him to communicate with more widely than if he had written only in Igbo. (Source)

Steaminess Rating

PG

Prostitution, sleeping with a forbidden love, abortion…there is sex in *No Longer At Ease*, but it occurs off-stage. Nevertheless, we do see Clara and Obi talking (or fighting) in bed. We also witness Elsie Marks's offer of sex with Obi in exchange for a promise that Obi will help her appear before the Scholarship Board. Ultimately, Obi does begin to sleep with girls who hope that it will help their chances of getting a scholarship to study in England. But each of these scenes hardly crosses over the line even into PG-13.

Allusions and Cultural References

Literature and Philosophy

- Matthew 4:16, King James Version (1.41)
- Proverbs 9:10, King James Version (1.48)
- T.S. Eliot, "The Love Song of J. Alfred Prufrock" (2.25)
- Isaiah 7:3 (3.39)
- Samuel Taylor Coleridge, "The Rime of the Ancient Mariner" (3.48)
- Graham Greene, Tutuola (5.4)
- Graham Greene, *The Heart of the Matter* (5.5 & 5.8)
- W.H. Auden (5.11)
- Evelyn Waugh, *A Handful of Dust* (5.11)
- An excerpt from the Gloria Patri, sometimes referred to as the Doxology (5.88; 5.90)
- Matthew 25.1-13, Parable of the Ten Virgins (6.49)
- Psalm 133.1 (8.30)
- The Book of Joel, *Bible* (10.2)
- Phrase "the day of the Lord": Isaiah 2:12; 13:6, 9; Ezekiel 13:5, 30:3; Joel 1:15, 2:1,11,31; 3:14; Amos 5:18,20; Obadiah 15; Zephaniah 1:7,14; Zechariah 14:1; Malachi. 4:5; Acts 2:20; 2 Thessalonians 2:2; 2 Peter 3:10. (10.3)
- A.E. Housman, *Collected Poems* (10.56; 16.28)
- Joseph Conrad, *Heart of Darkness* (11.12)
- Galatians 3.28 (14.33)
- 2 Kings 5:1-14 (14.36)
- Matthew 26:52 (14.60)
- 2 Samuel 12:15-20 (18.47)
- Philippians 4:7 (18.47)

Historical Figures

- Adolf Hitler (1.40, 4.61-62)
- Kaiser's war, i.e., World War I (7.2)

Best of the Web

Videos

Interview with Chinua Achebe
http://www.youtube.com/watch?v=msvHApfM_3A
Oyiza Adaba interviews Chinua Achebe for the 50th anniversary of Achebe's famous novel *Things Fall Apart*.

Chinua Achebe
http://www.youtube.com/watch?v=IYEVOe646gI
Presentation at the Christopher Okigbo International Conference at Harvard University

Chinua Achebe Interview
http://www.youtube.com/watch?v=iCic_RoPhoM
Bill Moyers interviews Chinua Achebe

Chinua Achebe Interview
http://www.youtube.com/watch?v=mNdjcFOoVi8
Achebe talks about slavery, the African diaspora, Africa, and colonialism.

Audios

No Longer At Ease
http://www.youtube.com/watch?v=RBS5_DtVxO4
An album by Nneka.

Images

Chinua Achebe
http://reading.cornell.edu/reading_project_05/images/chinua_achebe.jpg
Poster for a reading at Cornell.

Documents

A Long Way From Home
http://www.guardian.co.uk/books/2007/jul/10/chinuaachebe
An interview with Chinua Achebe in *The Guardian*.

The New Black Magazine

http://www.thenewblackmagazine.com/view.aspx?index=589
The New Black Magazine reviews *No Longer At Ease*.

BBC Story on Chinua Achebe
http://www.bbc.co.uk/bbcfour/documentaries/profile/chinua-achebe.shtml
This is a great, short profile on Chinua Achebe. Plus, it links to other BBC articles about Nigeria and Achebe's disillusionment with Nigeria.

Chinua Achebe
http://www.collegenews.org/x7127.xml
Bard Professor wins Booker Prize

6847917R00056

Printed in Great Britain
by Amazon.co.uk, Ltd.,
Marston Gate.